W9-BUW-023

Combining Images
with Photoshop®
Elements

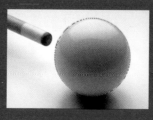

Combining Images
with **Photoshop**® Elements

Selecting, Layering, Masking,
and Compositing

Ted LoCascio

WILEY PUBLISHING, INC.

Acquisitions Editor: Pete Gaughan
Development Editor: James Compton
Technical Editor: Mark Clarkson
Production Editor: Daria Meoli
Copy Editor: Liz Welch
Production Manager: Tim Tate
Vice President and Executive Group Publisher: Richard Swadley
Vice President and Executive Publisher: Joseph B. Wikert
Vice President and Publisher: Dan Brodnitz
Permissions Editor: Shannon Walters
Media Development Specialist: Angela Denny
Book Designer: Lori Barra, Tonbo Design
Compositor: Franz Baumhackl
Proofreader: Jennifer Larsen, Word One
Indexer: Ted Laux
Cover Designer: Ryan Sneed
Cover Image: Ted LoCascio

Copyright © 2006 by Wiley Publishing, Inc., Indianapolis, Indiana

Published simultaneously in Canada

ISBN-13: 978-0-471-91863-9
ISBN-10: 0-471-91863-6

No part of this publication may be reproduced, stored in a retrieval system
or transmitted in any form or by any means, electronic, mechanical, photo-
copying, recording, scanning or otherwise, except as permitted under Sections
107 or 108 of the 1976 United States Copyright Act, without either the prior
written permission of the Publisher, or authorization through payment of
the appropriate per-copy fee to the Copyright Clearance Center, 222
Rosewood Drive, Danvers, MA 01923, (978) 750-8400, fax (978) 646-
8600. Requests to the Publisher for permission should be addressed to
the Legal Department, Wiley Publishing, Inc., 10475 Crosspoint Blvd.,
Indianapolis, IN 46256, (317) 572-3447, fax (317) 572-4355, or online
at http://www.wiley.com/go/permissions.

Limit of Liability/Disclaimer of Warranty: The publisher and the author make
no representations or warranties with respect to the accuracy or completeness
of the contents of this work and specifically disclaim all warranties, including without limitation warranties of fitness for a particular purpose. No
warranty may be created or extended by sales or promotional materials.
The advice and strategies contained herein may not be suitable for every sit-
uation. This work is sold with the understanding that the publisher is not
engaged in rendering legal, accounting, or other professional services. If
professional assistance is required, the services of a competent professional
person should be sought. Neither the publisher nor the author shall be
liable for damages arising herefrom. The fact that an organization or Website is referred to in this work as a citation and/or a potential source of further information does not mean that the author or the publisher endorses
the information the organization or Website may provide or recommenda-
tions it may make. Further, readers should be aware that Internet Websites
listed in this work may have changed or disappeared between when this
work was written and when it is read.

For general information on our other products and services or to obtain
technical support, please contact our Customer Care Department within
the U.S. at (800) 762-2974, outside the U.S. at (317) 572-3993 or fax
(317) 572-4002.

Wiley also publishes its books in a variety of electronic formats. Some content that appears in print may not be available in electronic books.

Library of Congress Cataloging-in-Publication Data is available from the
publisher.

TRADEMARKS: Wiley, the Wiley logo, and the Sybex logo are trademarks or registered trademarks of John Wiley & Sons, Inc. and/or its
affiliates, in the United States and other countries, and may not be used
without written permission. Photoshop is a registered trademark of Adobe
Systems Incorporated in the United States and/or other countries. All
other trademarks are the property of their respective owners. Wiley Publishing, Inc., is not associated with any product or vendor mentioned in
this book.

Selected images are © PhotoSpin (www.PhotoSpin.com) and are used
by permission.

10 9 8 7 6 5 4 3 2 1

Dear Reader,

Thank you for choosing *Combining Images with Photoshop Elements.* This book is part of a family of quality Sybex graphics books, all written by outstanding authors who combine practical experience with a gift for teaching.

Sybex was founded in 1976. Thirty years later, we're committed to producing consistently exceptional books, written for professionals and aspiring professionals. With each of our graphics titles we're working hard to set a new standard for the industry. From the writers and artists we work with to the paper we print on, our goal is to bring you the best books in the business.

I hope you see all that reflected in these pages. I'd be very interested to hear your comments and get your feedback on how we're doing. To let us know what you think about this or any other Sybex graphics book, please send me an email at sybex_publisher @wiley.com. Please also visit us at www.sybex.com to learn more about the rest of our growing graphics line.

Best regards,

DAN BRODNITZ
Vice President and Publisher
Sybex, an Imprint of Wiley

For my son, Enzo,
whom I can never take enough pictures of

Acknowledgments

First and foremost, I must thank everyone at Sybex for making this book possible. Thanks to publisher Dan Brodnitz and to acquisitions editor Pete Gaughan for sharing my vision on this project and for being as genuinely enthusiastic about Photoshop Elements as I am. Thanks also to development editor Jim Compton for helping me develop this title and paying such close attention to the details, and to Mark Clarkson for acting as my technical editor and making sure every step, shortcut, and tip is correct.

Special thanks to my copyeditor, Liz Welch, for making this book read as well as it does. I must also thank my production editor, Daria Meoli, for working with me on the book's schedule and keeping everything on track. I would also like to thank compositor Franz Baumhackl for doing such a great job of laying out the book.

I must also thank Lynda Weinman, Michael Ninness, Garo Green, Jonathan Humfrey, Garrick Chow, and the rest of the wonderful staff at Lynda.com for allowing me to be a part of their excellent online instructor team, and for being so much fun to work with. Thanks also to the entire KW Media staff and all of the PhotoshopWorld instructors who inspired me to write and teach.

I would also like to thank the *InDesign* magazine staff, especially Terri Stone, David Blatner, and Anne-Marie Concepcion.

Thanks also to Photospin.com for allowing me to use their images in this book.

Loving thanks to my wife, Jill, and to my son, Enzo, for being so patient while I was busy writing this book. Thanks also to Mom, Dad, Val, Bob and Evelyn Innocenti, and the rest of my extended family for being so supportive.

A big thanks also goes out to my extremely supportive friends: Al Ward, Jan Kabili, Dave Korman, Jeff Wood, Aaron and Colleen Akers, Brian Merrill, Sonny John Sundstrom, Michael Hoag, Stan Arthur, and Finn and Jackie Walling.

I would also like to thank my cats—Ito, Chloe, Tobias, and Clinton—for forcing me to take breaks from my writing in order to play with them.

And, of course, thanks to Adobe for making such great software to write about.

About the Author

Ted LoCascio is a professional graphics designer and an expert in Photoshop, Photoshop Elements, InDesign, Illustrator, and QuarkXPress. He served as senior designer at KW Media and the National Association of Photoshop Professionals (NAPP) for several years, and he has created layouts and designs for many successful software training books, videos, and magazines. He is the author of *InDesign CS2 at Your Fingertips* and *The InDesign Effects Book*, has contributed articles to *Photoshop User* magazine and *InDesign* magazine, and has taught at PhotoshopWorld. Ted is also the video author of *InDesign CS2 Essential Training* and *Creative Suite 2 Integration: Print Project Workflow*, available at Lynda.com. He also teaches a Digital Graphics course at St. Petersburg College, in Seminole, Florida.

A graphics designer for more than ten years, Ted has had designs and illustrations featured in several national newsstand and trade magazines, such as *Photoshop User, Mac Design*, Nikon's *Capture User, Great Output, AAA Going Places*, and *Florida Trend*. As a professional designer, he has used Adobe software to create layouts for magazines, books, and various advertising and marketing materials, including brochures, product packaging, posters and signs, and interactive PDFs.

A Chicago native (born a hopeless Cubs fan) and Columbia College alumnus, Ted relocated to the Tampa Bay area in 1994. He currently resides in Tarpon Springs, Florida, with his wife, Jill, and their son, Enzo.

Foreword

When you look at the wide selection of computer graphics titles in any bookstore (as you may be doing right now), you'll notice titles of all stripes. Some are strictly technical and read like the back of a medicine bottle. Others dazzle the eye with dynamic, full-color images but are light on actual content. Some books break everything down into "cookie cutter" recipes like a cookbook. There are books that try to encapsulate an entire software package and those that teach topic-specific areas of a program. With so many choices, what separates a quality book from the rest of the pack?

Two things make a great computer book stand out: the practicality of the material and the talent behind the keyboard leading the way. Where Adobe Photoshop Elements is concerned, Ted LoCascio is one of the few authors I know writing about the software who have the characteristics of a great teacher and can transfer that knowledge to a page. Ted is an expert in computer-aided design with years of professional training experience under his belt, and it shows. Not just the know-how comes through, though. Ted doesn't write simply *for* his readers, he writes *to* his reader. Whether Ted is explaining the tricks behind making quality selections, mastering masks, or creating fanciful filter effects, you get the feeling that Ted is sitting next to you guiding you through each topic, fully invested in your understanding of the material at hand. With this book you are getting more than simply the written word: Ted is also a dynamic video trainer, and the CD comes packed with additional video training by Ted himself.

I've known "of" Ted for a number of years, but over the past couple I've had the privilege of his friendship as well. If you want more from Elements than "the basics;" if you truly desire to learn the nuts and bolts of how to really make your workflow shine, then buy *Combining Images with Photoshop Elements* and let Ted guide you through. You will be well rewarded.

AL WARD
Action Fx Photoshop Resources: Home of 13,000+ Photoshop and Elements Presets
http://actionfx.com
Author, *Photoshop for Right-Brainers: The Art of Photo Manipulation*, Sybex

Contents

Chapter 3   Modifying Selections

Chapter 4   Mastering Layers

Chapter 8 **Adding Filters, Styles, and Effects** 225

"The deeper
you dig,

the more creative

you can get."

Introduction

I've been using Photoshop since the early '90s, and one of
my absolute favorite things to do with the application is to
combine images. Whether I have a specific story to tell or I
am searching for something new to create, I find no task
more enjoyable than compositing. Thankfully, I'm not alone
in my love for combining images, and with this book I am
sharing some of my favorite techniques as applied to
Photoshop Elements.

When my editors approached me about creating this book for Photoshop Elements
rather than for Photoshop CS2, I had serious reservations. How could the inexpensive
"baby brother" application even come close to the mighty Photoshop for combining
images? But once I started exploring in Elements, I soon realized that there is a lot more
you can do with this application than most of us are aware of. The deeper you dig, the
more creative you can get. In this book, I show you how to combine images using layers,
masks, brushes, gradients, and more.

Each year as new versions of Photoshop Elements are released, more and more
features are added, and that makes image compositing even more compelling to the
consumer-level digital photo enthusiast. If our friends at Adobe keep up this pattern,
we have a lot to look forward to in the years to come.

Who Should Use This Book

Although anyone with an interest in image compositing can benefit from this book, it
was written with the following three audiences in mind:

Digital Photography enthusiasts who are looking to expand their knowledge of
Photoshop Elements and create their own works of art. Yes, it's true. There is a
lot more you can do with your images in Elements than simply applying automated
color adjustments.

Fine artists and photographers who are seeking new and creative ways to combine digital images and produce great prints of their work.

Creative directors and graphics designers looking for an affordable tool they can use to create composite images for design clients. With certain limitations (e.g., CMYK conversion), it is possible to integrate Elements into your workflow. As long as you have at least one copy of Photoshop CS2 in your production department, you can convert your Elements client composites to CMYK. You can then import the converted artwork into a page layout program such as Adobe InDesign or QuarkXPress.

What's Inside

Combining Images with Photoshop Elements walks you through the entire compositing process, from concept to completion. Many of the chapters contain example projects in which each step is clearly outlined. I encourage you to try these procedures using your own files. Here is a brief description of what each chapter covers:

Chapter 1: It All Starts with an Idea explores the many different ways to find artistic inspiration and discover your own unique creative process.

Chapter 2: Making Good Selections helps you explore all of the selection tools, making it much easier to identify which ones are best for the selection at hand.

Chapter 3: Modifying Selections explains how to add pixels to or subtract pixels from a selection, as well as how to soften a selection edge and how to save selections for later use in a composition.

Chapter 4: Mastering Layers shows you how to edit, move, blend, fine-tune, and transform each element of your composition using layers. Layer navigation and management principles are explained in detail, and layer types are defined.

Chapter 5: The Power of Opacity and Blending takes a much closer look at the Layers palette and explores how it can be used to adjust the opacity value for individual layers in a composition. It also explains how you can control the way layers interact with one another by applying different blend modes.

Chapter 6: Compositing with Masks explains how to composite nondestructively using layer masks with brushes, gradients, filters, and filled selections. It also shows how to use clipping masks to place images inside text characters or other shapes.

Chapter 7: Advanced Masking with Camera RAW takes a look at how to use layer masks with Camera RAW files to combine enhanced shadow/highlight information and color temperature adjustments.

Chapter 8: Adding Filters, Styles, and Effects offers some creative ways to apply filters, layer styles, and effects to your combined image projects.

The Companion CD

On the companion CD that comes with *Combining Images with Photoshop Elements*, you'll find a selection of QuickTime training movies that accompany the lessons outlined in Chapters 2 through 8. The following is a list of the movies, organized by chapter as they appear named on the CD:

Chapter 2: Making Good Selections

- 02_01_rectangular_marquee.mov
- 02_02_magnetic_lasso.mov
- 02_03_magic_wand.mov
- 02_04_magic_extractor.mov

Chapter 3: Modifying Selections

- 03_01_feather.mov
- 03_02_save_selections.mov

Chapter 4: Mastering Layers

- 04_01_selecting_layers.mov
- 04_02_adjustment_layers.mov

Chapter 5: The Power of Opacity and Blending

- 05_01_applied_blending.mov

Chapter 6: Compositing with Masks

- 06_01_masks&filled_selections.mov
- 06_02_gradient_masks.mov
- 06_03_painting_in_masks.mov
- 06_04_type_masks.mov

Chapter 7: Advanced Masking with Camera RAW

- 07_01_shadow&highlight.mov

Chapter 8: Adding Filters, Styles, and Effects

- 08_01_filter_gallery_oilpaint.mov

How to Contact the Author

I am always happy to answer any questions that you may have about Photoshop Elements. If you can't find the answer in this book, please e-mail your question to ted@lukasnmc.com.

Sybex strives to keep you supplied with the latest tools and information you need for your work. Please check www.sybex.com for any additional content or updates that supplement this book. Enter the book's ISBN (0471918636) in the Search box, or type **combining elements**; then click Go to get to the book's update page.

It All Starts with an Idea

A little bit of imagination can take you a long way with Photoshop Elements. There are so many different ways to combine images that you may not know where to start. You may be asking yourself, "What types of images should I use? Where can I search for ideas?" Well, the truth is that these answers come from within. Photoshop Elements is an amazing tool with many automated features, but combining images is not one of them. By its very nature, combining images—compositing—is a task that can't be automated. It requires us to begin with an idea of the goal to be achieved and to make a series of evolving decisions about how to achieve that goal. Now's your chance to show your creative side! In this chapter, we'll explore different ways to find artistic inspiration and discover your own unique creative process.

1

Elements can also be used as a professional tool to create composite images for design clients. This involves developing the client's idea, or in some cases, helping the client find an idea to work with and bringing it to life with your image. As long as you have at least one copy of Photoshop CS2 in your production department, you can convert your Elements client composites to CMYK. You can then import the converted artwork into a page layout program such as Adobe InDesign or QuarkXPress.

This chapter also introduces two topics that are important for readers who are just getting started manipulating digital images: the basics of image resolution and sizing, and the RGB color mode. (More advanced Elements users can skim these sections or jump ahead to Chapter 2, "Making Good Selections.") By the end of this chapter, you'll be overflowing with ideas and ready to start compositing.

The Creative Process

I'm sure you've heard the phrase "Every picture tells a story," or "A picture is worth a thousand words." Well, there's a reason these sayings have been around for so long—*because they're true!* Images do tell stories, and creating them in Photoshop Elements *makes you a storyteller.*

As a storyteller, you need to understand that every image you create has its own personal meaning for you as the artist, but it may not have the same meaning for those who view it. Your story can be interpreted in lots of different ways. That's what makes creating images in this way so powerful.

Telling Your Story

So how do you go about telling these stories? What if you don't have a story to tell?

You always have a story to tell, even if you don't know what it is yet. Some of my best collage work *just happens.* (Figures 1.1 through 1.4 show a typical sequence, from the starting image to the finished montage.) As you work, it's easy to become immersed in the image you're creating, and before you know it the story begins to tell itself. Every layer, mask, brush stroke, and blend mode that you add to your image also adds to your story. The key is to not be too self-critical. The more comfortable you get with the tools for combining images in Photoshop Elements, the easier it is for you to follow your creative impulses and experiment. Don't be afraid to explore your every idea.

Figure 1.1
Before I created the final montage shown in Figure 1.4, I knew I wanted to work with this flower photograph, but I wasn't sure what other images to use with it.

Figure 1.2
I decided to bypass the creative roadblock and began extracting the flower from its background using the Magic Extractor in Photoshop Elements 4. (You'll learn how to work with this tool in Chapter 2 and the related lesson on the CD.)

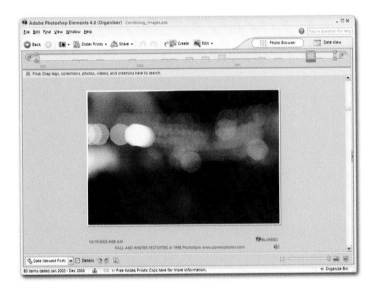

Figure 1.3
Once I had the flower image on its own layer, I began browsing through the photos in my Organizer Catalog (Windows) or Bridge (Mac). When I found this blurry city image, something just connected. The images are similar in color yet totally different in subject matter. It occurred to me that combining these two images might create an interesting contrast. I found my background!

Figure 1.4
Once I trusted my eye and refused to limit myself with specific expectations, the image essentially created itself.

Some images tell stories that are more straightforward than others. Not every project that combines images in Photoshop Elements has to be an abstract montage or collage. For example, you may want to combine images that create a visual document of a special moment in your life, such as a family vacation, a birthday, or a wedding (see Figure 1.5).

Figure 1.5
This wedding montage combines three different images, all brought together using layers, gradient masks, and brushwork.

You can also combine images in Photoshop Elements to change the mood or feeling of an existing photo (see Figure 1.6). These kinds of projects tend to inspire viewers and suggest underlying stories. It's amazing how much you can change the mood of a photograph just by replacing its background.

Before   After

Figure 1.6 The photo of the giraffe on the left is nice, but I thought it could use something more. I decided to replace the blue background with one of a clouded sky. Doing so creates a much more playful, dreamlike mood when viewing the image. For some, viewing the revised image may evoke memories of childhood.

Getting Inspired

Keep in mind that every storyteller's journey is unique, and what inspires me creatively may not inspire you. It's up to you to find out what ignites your creative spark.

There are a lot of things you can do to get into a creative mind-set. Here are some sources of inspiration that may work for you:

Books and magazines Try visiting your local library or bookstore and browsing through some fine art and photography books and magazines. Take note of which colors and textures catch your eye; you can use them later in your own projects.

Inspiration vs. Imitation

It is considered copyright infringement to directly imitate another artist's composition. However, there is absolutely nothing wrong with another artist's work inspiring you to create original work of your own. For more information, visit www.copyright.gov/title37/ or www.copyright.com.

Museums and galleries It can be very inspiring to visit a museum or gallery and look at the artwork up close. Make a mental note of the colors and brush strokes that speak loudest to you. Don't limit yourself to art museums; you might also find inspiration at a science or history museum. When visiting them, bring a sketchbook and make some quick drawings of the objects that interest you most.

Travel Taking a trip can be a great way to find artistic inspiration. Visiting new places and experiencing new things can suggest new stories for you to tell with your combined image projects. You may not even have to travel very far. In fact, your local park could be a source of inspiration. Wherever you go, be sure to bring a camera so that you can document all of the interesting new things you encounter. You may be able to use these photos in a montage or collage (see Figure 1.7).

Have Camera, Will Travel

If you bring a digital camera on a trip, remember to bring a backup battery and a few extra memory cards (or a portable storage drive). This way, you'll always be ready to snap a picture whenever you encounter something interesting that catches your eye.

Figure 1.7 I was able to snap the shot on the top while sailing along the Florida Intracoastal canal on a catamaran. As the sun began to set, I noticed the clouds beginning to glow and I raced for my camera. Only a couple of minutes later, the glow of the clouds was gone, as evidenced by the shot on the bottom. The window of opportunity to take this photograph was very small. Thankfully, by being prepared and having my camera with me, I was able to capture the moment perfectly.

Scrapbooks   Take time to browse through some old magazines or newspapers that you might have lying around the house. Be sure to bookmark any interesting photos, layouts, or type treatments. You can also tear out the pages that inspire you and keep them in a scrapbook. This way, you can always refer to them later whenever you need motivation.

Classes   Taking a class in fine art or computer design can be a great source of inspiration. Not only can you brush up on your skills and find encouragement through your instructor, but you can also interact with other artists. You'd be surprised how much the person sitting next to you in class can influence your work.

Not all your inspiration will come through your eyes, and it's equally important to prepare yourself mentally for creative activity:

Music   For some artists, listening to music is a great way to get into a creative mind-set. If music inspires you, try putting on your favorite CD or iTunes playlist and browsing through the images in your Photoshop Elements Organizer (Windows) or Bridge application (Mac). Before you know it, you'll be combining images in the Editor and creating your next masterpiece!

Exercise   It's always a good idea to free your mind and body from everyday stress before starting a new creative project, and for some, there's no better way to do this than through exercise. Try taking a jog, a walk, or a swim, or completing a 30-minute workout. It may energize you creatively as well as physically.

Day-to-day activities   Simple everyday activities such as cooking, gardening, or home decorating can also be great stress relievers that can help prepare and inspire you for your next creative project.

Staying Inspired

Getting inspired is the easy part. The real challenge comes with trying to *stay* inspired and avoiding those creative "blocks." Here are some suggestions:

Avoid expectations   To avoid falling into a creative rut, it helps if you go into a project without any expectations. Your original idea, or your client's idea, may not work out as planned, and this can be very frustrating. It's better to always keep the creativity flowing and allow your project to change and develop as you work on it. If you're working with a client on a project, be sure to keep the communication channels open and always explain *why* a certain idea is not working. Do your best to train your clients to avoid expectations just as you do.

Always have a backup plan   Rather than beating a project that isn't working into the ground, make sure you have some other ideas that you can try. It's best to have as many options as possible. This way, if things don't work out as planned, you can always move on to the next idea without getting frustrated. Just let it go and begin exploring something else.

Don't limit yourself   Be as open as possible and try every idea that pops into your head. Experiment as much as possible with the images you are working with. Try a blend mode you've never used before, or mix up the layer order just to see what happens. The more you play, the more likely you are to stumble across what I like to call a "happy accident." You never know—you may discover a new technique that you can use over and over again with other projects.

Take breaks   Compositing with Photoshop Elements can become addicting. The more you work, the faster time disappears. Just remember, as you stare into the computer screen trying to create the perfect collage—you still have a life, *and it may be passing you by*. Take a break every once in a while and do something else. Not only will your friends and family members appreciate it, but you'll also be giving yourself a chance to clear your head. Later, when you return to your project, you'll have a fresh new perspective that can add to the overall creative excitement of your image.

Gathering Images

Before you can start compositing in Photoshop Elements, you first need some images to combine. There are several ways to collect images for compositing. You can take your own photographs, scan in "found objects," or collect stock images from royalty-free subscription services.

You may have a certain composition in mind before you begin compositing. If so, it's up to you to stage the photo shoot, find the objects you're looking for and scan them in, or locate royalty-free stock images that match your description.

If you do not have a particular composition in mind, then you'll most likely be using whatever images speak to you at the moment. Sometimes this can be a much more creative and fun way to work, but it helps to have a backlog of images to choose from in your Elements Catalog (Windows) or on your drive (Mac).

So where can you find exciting images to use in your projects? What types of images should you look for? Believe it or not, images are everywhere. All you need to do is start looking for them. All around you are images that can inspire new compositing projects.

The Power of Observation

Once you begin combining images with Photoshop Elements, you'll most likely discover a whole new way of looking at the world around you. You may find yourself always looking for images to include in compositing projects. If so, try to always keep a camera with you. This way, you'll always be ready to snap a picture whenever something exciting catches your eye. As Figure 1.8 shows, abstract forms that lend themselves to compositing can be found almost anywhere.

Figure 1.8
It's worth taking the time to capture the details of the world around you. Here, I couldn't resist photographing the way the oil drops separated in the glass of water. It struck me as a great image to base a compositing project around later.

Image Resources

There are many places where you can find images to include in your combined image projects. Here are some resources that you may want to explore:

Thrift shops, flea markets, and antique stores Collage artists tend to be what I call "image pack rats." We just love to poke around in thrift shops, flea markets, and antique stores looking for the next unique object to include in an image. These shops can be virtual treasure chests full of ideas. You can either purchase the items that speak to you most and photograph them later, or, if you've already got a house filled with way too many "found objects," bring a camera with you and—with the owner's permission, of course—photograph the items right in the store (see Figure 1.9).

Figure 1.9
I photographed these starfish at an outdoor market in my hometown of Tarpon Springs, Florida. I was intrigued by their intricate texture—something I might be able to use in a future combined image project.

In the street/in your yard Although they may seem like unlikely places to collect images for compositing, the street outside and even your own backyard can be among the best resources for "found objects." A found object is any interesting item that you happen to stumble across that can later be incorporated into a combined image project, such as the butterfly wings shown in Figure 1.10.

Figure 1.10
I found these butterfly wings on my back patio. I quickly gathered them up, photographed them, and scanned them in. What a score!

Family albums/old photos Old family photos can be great for combined image projects. In fact, in some cases—the older, the better. You can scan these images and use them to create a montage that tells a story about the past and how it relates to the present or future, or you can create a collage that tells a story about your family history (see Figure 1.11).

Royalty-free stock agencies For commercial projects you may need to find a specific image. Not to worry. There are plenty of royalty-free stock photo agencies out there that you can purchase photos from. Many of them offer CD collections that you can buy, and most of them also offer affordable subscription memberships that allow you to search an online database and download images from a website at low, medium, and high resolutions. Figure 1.12 shows one agency's website.

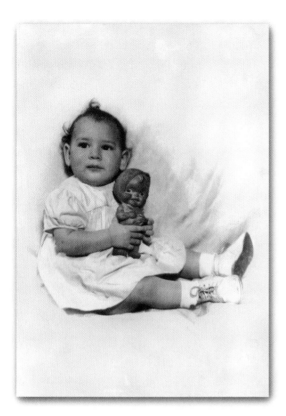

Figure 1.11
This photo was taken in 1950.
Photography sure has come a
long way since then.

Figure 1.12
Photospin.com is
one of my favorite
resources for
royalty-free stock
imagery.

Understanding Resolution

Before you get started with compositing, it's important to know how to size your images,
and that requires working with *image resolution*. Understanding resolution allows you
take greater control over the final size of your combined image projects. Scaling your finished images to the exact size and resolution you want is the best possible way to ensure

that you will always get high-quality prints. If you are creating a project exclusively for onscreen display, it ensures that you won't be wasting hard drive space by using more pixels than you need.

 Tip: If you're already familiar with the basic pixel arithmetic of image resolution and sizing, feel free to jump to Chapter 2, "Making Good Selections."

Pixel Logic

Every digital image that you open in Photoshop Elements is made up of thousands, or even millions of tiny, square pixels. The closer you zoom in on an image, the more visible these individual square pixels become onscreen (see Figure 1.13). A pixel is the fundamental building block of a digital image. Each of the binary numbers that make up an image file represents the color of a single pixel, which is the value recorded from a single cell on the digital camera's sensor chip. The camera's resolution ultimately determines the maximum resolution an image can have, but for most forms of output you'll work at a lower resolution.

Figure 1.13
By zooming in to 1600%, you can begin to see the square pixels that make up this image.

Image resolution is determined by the number of pixels per inch (ppi for short) that an image contains. This is the measurement that tells us what each image's print size and quality will be upon output. To ensure that you will get a good print of your image, you need to first check the current resolution and document size before printing.

Although the default, suggested print resolution in Elements is 300 ppi, modern studies prove that an image really only needs to be 220 ppi at 100% of its intended print size to produce a high-quality print. If you are creating an image to be displayed on the Web or exclusively onscreen, the image resolution should be set to 72 ppi at 100% of its intended viewing size.

For example, an image that is 3×2.4 inches at a resolution of 220 ppi can produce a high-quality print, but contains more pixels than is needed for web display (web images should be as small as possible so that they can download quickly into a browser). The same 3×2.4 image at a resolution of only 72 ppi is small enough to display on the Web and to send as an e mail attachment, but cannot produce a high-quality print (see Figure 1.14).

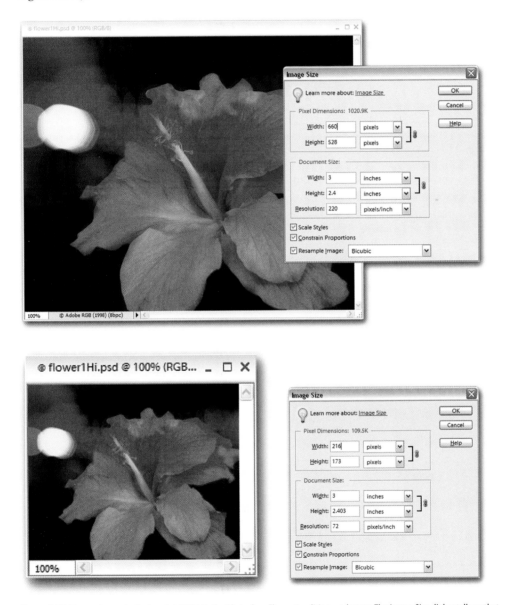

Figure 1.14 The top image is displayed at 100% in the Photoshop Elements editing workspace. The Image Size dialog tells us that it is 3" wide by 2.4" tall at a resolution of 220 dpi. For the lower image we've kept the dimensions at 3×2.4" and changed the resolution to 72 dpi. Notice that the onscreen display, as well as the pixel dimensions and the overall file size (shown at the top of the Image Size dialog), are significantly smaller for the lower image than they are for the top image.

When photographing an image for print, be sure to use the medium or large capture setting on your digital camera. Doing so allows enough resolution to produce a high-quality print at a normal output size. Most consumer-level digital cameras save captured images at a universal resolution of 72 ppi; however, at medium and large capture settings the pixel dimensions are increased, allowing for higher-quality output.

When scanning an image for print, be sure to import the image at 100%, using a minimum setting of 220 ppi.

 Note: If you're not sure how large you want to use an image in a compositing project, always photograph or scan it using a higher input setting. Remember, you can always downsample to a lower resolution, but you can't upsample to a higher resolution.

What's My Resolution?

By default, Photoshop Elements displays the current image dimensions in inches at the bottom-left corner of the document window, with the current image resolution shown at the end in parenthesis. By clicking and holding the left mouse button down on this value, you can access a pop-up window that displays the image width and height in pixels, as well as the number of channels (3 for an RGB image), and the current image resolution.

You can change the information that is displayed in the lower-left corner of the document window by clicking the black arrow to the right of the field. Choose another option from the pop-up menu, such as the color profile that is currently applied, or the tool that you currently have selected.

Elements uses inches as the default measurement for displaying document dimensions, but you can change this in the Units And Rulers panel of the Preferences dialog. Choose Edit > Preferences > Units And Rulers (Windows) or Photoshop Elements > Preferences > Units and Rulers (Mac), and select your preferred unit of measurement from the Rulers menu. To better understand resolution and image sizing, choose Pixels rather than Inches as you're working in this book. This can help you to start thinking of your images in terms of pixels, which is ultimately what you are working with.

You can also choose a different unit of measurement from the Cursor Coordinates pop-up menu available in the Info palette. Choose Window > Info to display the palette, then click and hold the + next to the X/Y coordinates in the bottom left to access the menu.

Changing the default unit of measurement in either location changes the measurement that is displayed at the bottom left of the document window and at the bottom of the Info palette (when it's visible).

Controlling the Info Palette Display

You can choose what document information you'd like displayed at the bottom of the Info palette. Choose Palette Options from the Info palette menu and check your preferred options at the bottom of the Options dialog:

You can choose as many or as few as you like. Click OK to apply. The Info palette here has been modified to display all status information:

Resizing Images

You can access image size and resolution information and make any necessary adjustments using the Image Size dialog. To display the dialog, choose Image > Resize > Image Size or press Alt+Ctrl+I (Windows) or Opt+⌘+I (Mac) (see Figure 1.15).

Figure 1.15

The top of the Image Size dialog displays the overall file size as well as the image width and height dimensions in pixels. The center of the dialog displays the current document size using the measurement of your choice (the default unit is inches), as well as the current image resolution value in pixels per inch.

With the Resample Image option checked, you can raise or lower the resolution value while maintaining the current document size. Lowering the resolution (called *downsampling*) decreases the pixel dimensions of the image by removing pixels and reduces the overall file size (see Figure 1.16). Increasing the resolution value (called *upsampling*) adds pixels to the image and increases the file size (see Figure 1.17). When compositing, you will most likely be downsampling your images rather than upsampling. Downsampling is a great way to resize large images before compositing them into a single document.

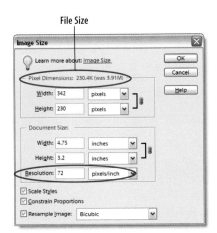

Figure 1.16 Downsampling from 300 ppi to 72 ppi; notice that the file size displayed at the top of the dialog has been reduced.

Figure 1.17 Upsampling from 300 ppi to 600 ppi; notice that the file size displayed at the top of the dialog has been increased.

With the Resample Image option deselected, you can raise or lower the resolution value and alter the document size while maintaining the current pixel dimensions. In other words, you can resize an image this way without adding or removing pixels. Doing so does not alter the file size or create a noticeable change in the image when viewed on screen. It only affects the document size and the quality of the image when printing (see Figure 1.18).

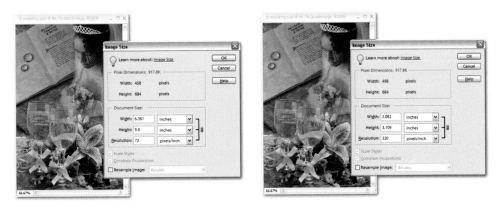

Figure 1.18 Left: The original 72 ppi image. Right: In order to get a high-quality print from this image, you must deselect the Resample Image option in the Image Size dialog and increase the resolution value to at least 220 ppi. Doing so outputs the image at a much smaller print size

Note: To produce a high-quality print of your project, make sure that your images are large enough to print at the intended size *and* are at least 220 ppi. It helps to size your images appropriately ahead of time; otherwise, they may be too small to include in your project.

RGB Color Mode

Photoshop Elements allows you to edit color images using RGB color mode. The letters stand for Red-Green-Blue, named for each color channel available in this mode. Every pixel in an image is made up of a percentage of grayscale information contained in each of these color channels. Photoshop Elements uses these percentages to calculate the amount of red, green, and blue light that make up the colors you see onscreen. Any edits you make to the image actually alter the information contained in all three color channels.

When compositing images in Elements, you will predominantly be working with 8-bit RGB images, which offers you 256 tonal variations in each RGB component. That amounts to almost 16 million possible colors! If that's not enough for you, you can also work with 16-bit RGB images, which greatly multiply the number of colors available, but also greatly increase your file size. Also, keep in mind that several important editing tools and functions required for compositing, such as layers, are not available when working with 16-bit images.

Color Settings

Before you start compositing, it makes sense to choose your preferred color management settings. Color management is intended to ensure that the colors you are viewing onscreen are displaying—as accurately as possible—a true representation of what your project will look like upon final output. The idea here is to maintain color consistency on every device (print and display) through the use of embedded color profiles. Color profiles are data files that describe the color behavior of a specific device. They act as a set of instructions that a device, such as a monitor or scanner, refers to in order to display color accurately.

A good way to start out with color management is to first calibrate your monitor. Calibration adjusts the output of your monitor to ensure accurate display. This is achieved by fine-tuning the brightness, contrast, and color balance settings.

You should take advantage of the Adobe Gamma software that is installed with Photoshop Elements. Choose Start > Settings > Control panel and double-click the Adobe Gamma icon. From here, you can use the Adobe Gamma Step-By-Step Wizard to assist you. Mac OS X users can calibrate using the Display Calibrator Assistant that comes with OS X. In System Preferences, choose Displays; click Color; then click the Calibrate button. The Assistant will walk you through the process from here.

If you're using a CRT monitor (as opposed to an LCD), you may also want to consider investing in a hardware calibration device, such as the Spyder by ColorVision. These hardware devices tend to be much more accurate than software calibration, since they do not rely on your eye as the above-mentioned software utilities do. Nowadays, some self-calibrating CRT monitors even ship with one of these devices.

Once it has calibrated your monitor, Adobe Gamma generates an ICC profile that Photoshop Elements can recognize on your system. You can then decide how you'd like to use color profiles with your images—or if you'd even like to use color management at all. For a more in-depth look at calibration and color management, you might want to check out Tim Grey's *Color Confidence* book (Sybex, 2004).

Since there are so many different monitors and printers available, there is no one specific way to manage color. It's up to you to run some tests on your images and choose the color settings that produce the most accurate and consistent results. You can choose these settings from the Color Settings dialog. To display the dialog, choose Edit > Color Settings or press Shift+Ctrl+K (Windows) or Shift+⌘+K (Mac) (see Figure 1.19).

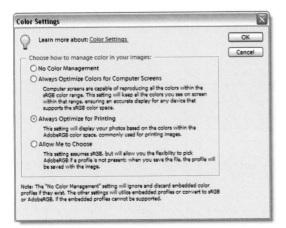

Figure 1.19
The Color Settings dialog

No Color Management   This is the default setting for Photoshop Elements. If you don't want to use color management, keep this setting enabled and don't make any changes in the dialog. Doing so tells Elements to ignore the existing profile when opening an image. With this option, choosing File > Save will not embed a profile. As a partial alternative, however, choosing File > Save As gives you the option to embed your monitor profile. Select the Embed Color Profile check box at the bottom of the Save As dialog to embed the ICC color profile created for your monitor (see Figure 1.20).

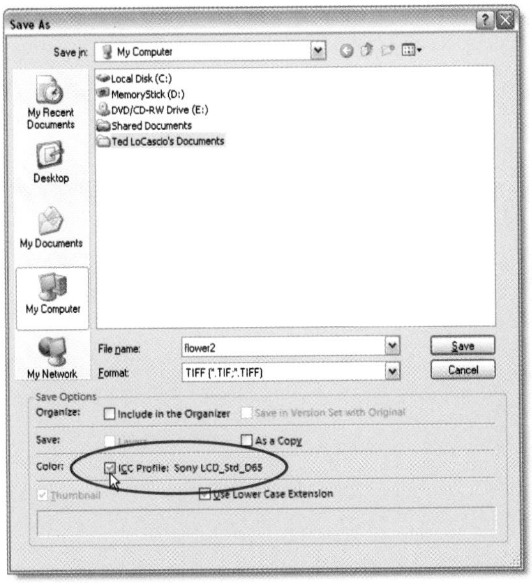

Figure 1.20
Even if you have selected No Color Management, the Save As window gives you the option of embedding your monitor's ICC color profile with an image.

Always Optimize Colors For Computer Screens   In previous versions of Photoshop Elements, this setting was called Limited Color Management. This is because it uses the sRGB limited color space. sRGB has a narrower range of colors (called a *gamut*), which is considered best for images intended for onscreen and web display. Choose this setting to apply sRGB as your default working space. Choosing File > Save does not embed the sRGB profile, but File > Save As gives you the option to do so. Select the Embed Color Profile check box at the bottom of the Save As dialog to embed the sRGB profile.

Always Optimize For Printing   In previous versions of Photoshop Elements, this option was called Full Color Management. This is because it uses the Adobe RGB color space. Adobe RGB has a wider gamut and therefore maps to a broader range of colors than sRGB. It is for this reason that Adobe considers it the best choice for color-managing images that are intended for print. Choosing this setting retains any existing profiles when opening an image. When you open images with no profile embedded, Elements applies the Adobe RGB profile. When you choose Save, the original profile is retained. Save As gives you the option not to embed the profile; simply deselect the Embed Color Profile check box at the bottom of the Save As dialog.

Allow Me To Choose   New to Photoshop Elements 4.0, this setting assumes sRGB, but allows you to choose whether to apply either sRGB or Adobe RGB when opening images that do not contain existing profiles. Choose File > Save to embed the chosen profile with the image.

All of this is a lot to take in for first-time Photoshop Elements users, so if your head is spinning, just choose the Always Optimize For Printing option. This way, you can ensure that all of your images are color-managed for print output. If you decide later to use an image exclusively for onscreen display, you can always convert the profile to sRGB.

Converting Profiles

To convert an image from one color profile to another, use the following steps:

1.   Close the image whose profile you want to convert.
2.   Press Shift+Ctrl+K (Windows) or Shift+⌘+K (Mac) to display the Color Settings dialog and change your color setting to No Color Management.

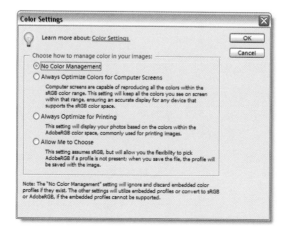

CHAPTER 1: IT ALL STARTS WITH AN IDEA ■

3. Reopen the untagged image. You can verify that it is untagged by choosing Document Profile from the pop-up menu in the lower-left corner of the document window.

4. To convert the image to sRGB, open the Color Settings dialog again and choose Always Optimize Colors For Computer Screens or Allow Me To Choose. To convert to Adobe RGB, open the Color Settings dialog again and choose Always Optimize For Printing.

5. Choose Save As and select the Embed Color Profile check box at the bottom of the Save As dialog. Click Save. When the warning dialog appears, click OK to save over the original image. The new profile is now embedded.

Making Good Selections

You now understand that combining images using Photoshop Elements means working with pixels. You can specify which images, or parts of images, you'd like to include in a montage or collage by selecting the pixels that define them. You can also use selections to identify any image layer areas that you'd like to mask. To make this task as painless as possible, Elements provides us with several tools for making "good" selections.

Chapter Contents

Defining "Good" Selections

So how can you tell whether a selection is "good?" It's simple. "Good" selections are made quickly, easily, and accurately. Therefore, it's worth taking the time to learn how to use all of the selection tools *before* getting started with your project. There are many types of selections you can make, and making them quickly, easily, and accurately requires the use of specific tools. Once you familiarize yourself with all of the tools, it will become much easier to identify which ones are best for making particular selections. Work smart, not hard—that's what I always say!

The Selection Border

One thing that nearly every selection has in common (with the exception of those made with the Magic Extract, Magic Eraser, and Background Eraser tools) is the selection border. This is Photoshop Elements' way of showing you that an area is selected. When you make a selection with the majority of these tools, a blinking dashed border appears around the selected area. This border is often referred to as "the marching ants," because it resembles a workforce of ants busily marching around your selection.

Once you've isolated an area, you can then move or manipulate it independently of the rest of the image. This is something you will do often when compositing.

> **Note:** Sometimes the marching ants can become very distracting. For example, to clearly see an effect that you'd like to apply to a selected area (such as a Gaussian blur), it helps if you hide the marching ants. Once you're confident that you've made an accurate selection, you can hide the ants by pressing Ctrl+H (Windows) or ⌘+H (Mac). You can then apply the effect without all of the distraction. To reveal the selection, press Ctrl / ⌘+H again.

The Tools Palette

By default, the Tools palette appears docked in a single column on the left side of your screen (see Figure 2.1). The Tools palette contains all the various tools available to you—each one represented by a descriptive icon. However, if you're still not sure what tool you're viewing, hover your mouse over it in the palette until a small tooltip description appears.

You can activate a tool by clicking its icon, or by typing its assigned keyboard shortcut (which is included in the tooltip). Any icon showing a small arrow in the bottom-right corner indicates an available toolset—more tools are "hidden" under the one shown. Clicking and holding the icon reveals a flyout menu of additional tools.

There are two ways to display the Tools palette on your screen. The default is the docked, single-column format, but by clicking at the top of the palette, holding the mouse button down, and dragging it away from the left side of your screen, you can change it to display in Adobe's traditional double-column format (see Figure 2.2).

To re-dock the Tools palette, simply click the top of the palette, hold the mouse button down, and drag it back to the left side of the screen.

Figure 2.1
The Tools palette in its default, docked state

Figure 2.2
The Tools palette when it is undocked

The Marquee Tools

You can use the marquee tools to select a fixed rectangular or elliptical region of an image. Want to include a picture of a window in your combined image project? How about a door? If so, then the Rectangular Marquee tool is your best bet. Or maybe you'd like to include an image of the moon? You guessed it. Use the Elliptical Marquee tool.

But if these simple geometric forms seem too limiting, don't worry. In fact, when combining images, there's also a lot more you can do with these tools than you may realize. You don't have to use the marquee tools exclusively for selecting image elements that are rectangular or elliptical in shape. It's also possible to use them to select portions of an image. Maybe you'd like to blend the top half of one photograph with the bottom half of another. You can do so using the Rectangular Marquee tool.

As you'll see in the following examples, the marquee selection tools can also be great for creating geometric shapes to be used in layer masks and clipping groups. For more on masking, see Chapter 6, "Compositing with Masks."

The Rectangular Marquee

The Rectangular Marquee tool selects a rectangular area of the image that you define by dragging diagonally from any corner. You access the Rectangular Marquee tool by clicking and holding the currently visible Marquee tool icon in the Tools palette and selecting

Rectangular Marquee Tool from the pop-up menu that appears (see Figure 2.3). You can also toggle between the Rectangular and Elliptical Marquee tools by pressing M.

To make a selection with the Rectangular Marquee tool, check the options bar, and make sure the Feather amount is set to 0px and Mode is set to Normal. Making a selection with a feathered value any higher than 0px adds a soft edge to the selection (for more on this, see Chapter 3, "Modifying Selections"). Then all you have to do is click the left mouse button and drag.

Figure 2.3
The Rectangular Marquee tool

 Note: The accompanying CD-ROM includes a video lesson on using the Rectangular Marquee selection tool.

Example: Framing a Photograph

Figures 2.4 through 2.8 demonstrate how I used the Rectangular marquee tool to frame a photograph inside the image of a film negative. (Note: This example will be easier to follow if you've already worked with layers.) Figure 2.4 shows the image as first opened in the Editor.

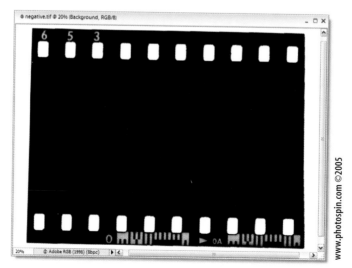

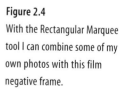
www.photospin.com ©2005

Figure 2.4
With the Rectangular Marquee tool I can combine some of my own photos with this film negative frame.

With the Rectangular Marquee tool, I was able to draw a rectangle selection where I wanted the photograph to appear (see Figure 2.5).

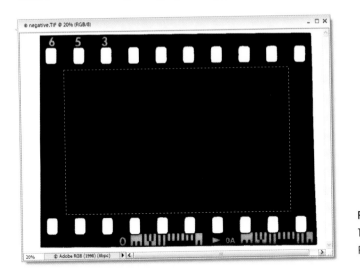

Figure 2.5
The image area is defined by the Rectangular Marquee tool selection.

My goal was to fill the selected area with a photograph, which required the use of a mask. Elements offers several adjustment layers that include layer masks. To gain access to a layer mask, I added a Levels adjustment layer without making any adjustments. To do so, I displayed the Layers palette by choosing Window > Layers, and then clicked the Adjustment Layer icon at the top of the palette and chose Levels (see Figure 2.6).

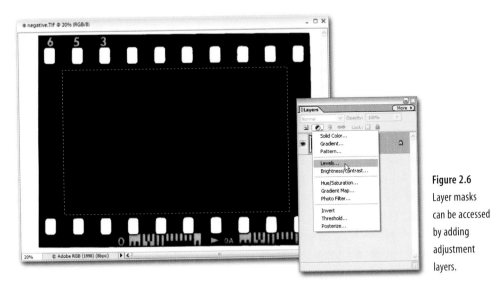

Figure 2.6
Layer masks can be accessed by adding adjustment layers.

The point here is not to make an actual Levels adjustment, but to gain access to the companion layer mask that automatically appears with the layer. I could just as easily have chosen the Hue And Saturation or Brightness/Contrast adjustment layers. All three of these adjustment layers feature a built-in layer mask, and even more important, won't affect my image if no adjustments are made.

Layer masks hide all or part of a layer. Anywhere the layer mask is black, the layer will be hidden. Where it is white, the layer will be revealed. Shades of gray partially hide the contents of the layer.

By adding the Levels (non)-adjustment layer, I was able to create a layer mask based on the rectangle selection. This allowed me to group additional imported images to the rectangle shape (see Figure 2.7). To achieve this effect, I placed an imported image on the layer above the masked (non)-adjustment layer and chose Layer > Group With Previous; I could also have pressed Ctrl+G (Windows) or ⌘+G (Mac).

Figure 2.7 A rectangular marquee selection, a layer mask, and a clipping group can be used to combine images nondestructively.

 Note: You can also group layers by Alt-clicking (Windows) or Opt-clicking (Mac) between layers in the Layers palette.

Additional images can be added to the group, allowing you to use the same frame effect for multiple photographs. In this example, I added several photos to the clipping group. I was then able to use the visibility controls in the Layers palette to display and ultimately print each photo in the film negative frame (see Figure 2.8).

Figure 2.8 Additional images can be added to the clipping group.

The Elliptical Marquee

You can access the Elliptical Marquee tool by clicking and holding the currently visible marquee tool icon in the Tools palette and selecting Elliptical Marquee Tool from the pop-up menu that appears (see Figure 2.9). You can also toggle between the Rectangular and Elliptical Marquee tools by pressing M.

To make a selection with the Elliptical Marquee tool, check the options bar and make sure Anti-alias is enabled, the Feather amount is set to 0px, and Mode is set to Normal. Then click and drag to make an elliptical selection.

Figure 2.9
The Elliptical
Marquee tool

Note: The Anti-alias option applies a slight transition between pixels, resulting in a smooth selection rather than a jagged one.

Example: An Elliptical Mask

With this example, I used the Elliptical marquee tool to mask one photograph inside another. With the cue ball image open, I drew an elliptical selection where I wanted another photograph to appear (see Figure 2.10).

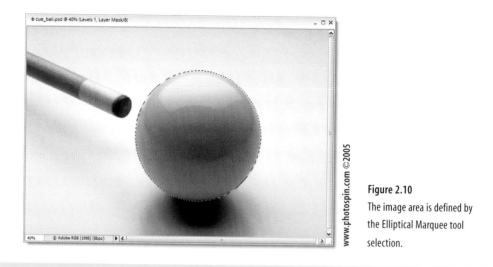

www.photospin.com ©2005

Figure 2.10
The image area is defined by the Elliptical Marquee tool selection.

Note: You can move a marquee selection path as you draw it by holding down the spacebar.

By applying the (non)-adjustment layer mask technique described earlier in "Framing a Photograph," I was able to create a layer mask based on my elliptical selection (see Figure 2.11). This allowed me to group the imported, tied-hands image to the circle shape. To outline the hands more closely, I then added to the mask by painting inside of it with a soft brush. For more on layer masks and grouping, see Chapter 6.

Figure 2.11
Using the Elliptical Marquee with masks and groups allowed me to create this montage.

Note: To draw an elliptical or rectangular selection from the center, hold down the Alt key (Windows) or Option key (Mac) as you click and drag. Once you begin drawing, add the Shift key to constrain width and height proportions. This allows you to create a perfect circle or square.

The Lasso Tools

The Lasso tool allows you to select intermittent portions of an image by tracing them in a freehand style. Sounds great, right? It is. Except for one major flaw—the tool is extremely difficult to control. Fortunately, Elements also includes Magnetic and Polygonal versions of the Lasso that can help guide your freeform selections. But the truth is that all three lasso tools are hard to trace with.

If you're new to the lasso tools, my recommendation is to start out by using them to select simple shapes—not detailed objects containing lots of intricate bends and curves. The simpler the shape you're trying to select, the easier it will be to trace with one of the Lassos. Keep in mind also that the more you draw with the lasso tools, the easier it will get. After a while, detailed selections will not seem as hard.

Note: If drawing freehand is your specialty, you might want to try using a graphics pen and tablet. Doing so can make tracing with the lasso tools much easier.

The Lasso Tool

In my experience, the Lasso is a much better tool for fine-tuning existing selections than for drawing new ones (a topic we'll explore further in Chapter 3). However, if you've got a steady hand and an incredible amount of patience, you can use the Lasso to make entire selections. For instance, you might consider using the Lasso tool to select the yellow blossom in Figure 2.12.

www.photospin.com ©2005

Figure 2.12 This flower stands out well from its background, so it seems to be a good candidate for tracing.

You can access the Lasso tool by clicking and holding the currently visible Lasso tool icon in the Tools palette and selecting Lasso Tool from the pop-up menu that appears (see Figure 2.13). You can also toggle between the Lasso, Magnetic Lasso, and Polygonal Lasso tools by pressing L.

Figure 2.13
The Lasso tool

 Note: You can also access the different lasso tools from the options bar.

To make a normal selection with the Lasso, check the options bar and make sure Anti-alias is selected and the Feather amount is set to 0px.

To make a freeform selection with the Lasso tool, click to create a starting point and proceed to trace around the image. Now, here's the tricky part: You must keep the mouse button pressed at all times while making the selection. If you release the mouse button early, Elements assumes that you have finished tracing and closes the selection path automatically (see Figure 2.14).

If you zoom in on the image before you begin tracing, you can make a much more precise selection (see Figure 2.15). As you trace, click and hold the spacebar to temporarily access the Hand tool and navigate around the image. This way, you don't have to let go of the mouse button and risk closing your selection early.

Note: As you trace with the traditional Lasso tool, you cannot zoom in or out on the image using the Ctrl and plus (+) or Ctrl and minus (-) (Windows) or ⌘ and plus (+) or ⌘ and minus (-) (Mac) keyboard shortcuts. Zooming in or out means letting up on the mouse button, which closes your selection before it is finished. This is why it is best to zoom in before you begin selecting with the tool.

Figure 2.14
Releasing the mouse button as you trace with the Lasso automatically closes your selection path.

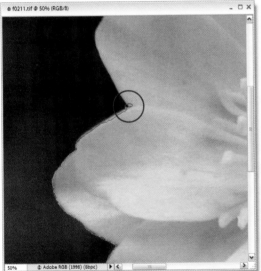

Figure 2.15
Zooming in on this yellow blossom made selecting it with the Lasso tool much easier.

The Magnetic Lasso Tool

The Magnetic Lasso tool offers you much more control for selecting entire objects than the traditional Lasso does. This version of the lasso automatically senses the edges of an object as you trace, even if the photograph contains low contrast and varied background colors. Because of this, the Magnetic Lasso tool is actually a much better tool for selecting the yellow blossom shown in Figure 2.12 than the Lasso.

Note: The accompanying CD-ROM includes a video lesson on using the Magnetic Lasso tool.

You can access the Magnetic Lasso tool by clicking and holding the currently visible Lasso tool icon in the Tools palette and selecting Magnetic Lasso Tool from the pop-up menu that appears (see Figure 2.16). You can also toggle between the Lasso, Magnetic Lasso, and Polygonal Lasso tools by pressing L.

Figure 2.16
The Magnetic Lasso tool

Note: Another way to toggle between the Lasso, Magnetic Lasso, and Polygonal Lasso tools is to Alt-click the currently visible Lasso tool icon in the Tools palette.

To make a normal selection with the Magnetic Lasso, check the options bar and make sure Anti-alias is selected and the Feather amount is set to 0px. Then click to create a starting point and proceed to trace around the edge of the image. The great thing about the Magnetic Lasso is that you do not need to keep the mouse button pressed as you trace—all you need to do is click once and move the mouse. Depending on your options bar settings and where the mouse is placed, Elements determines where the edge is and makes the selection for you. As you trace, the tool locks the line segments in place by automatically adding square anchor points to the selection path (see Figure 2.17).

Figure 2.17
Tracing with the Magnetic Lasso is much easier than tracing with the traditional Lasso tool.

The additional options bar settings allow you even greater control over the tool. The most significant of these is the Width option, which lets you set how close to the edge of the object your cursor needs to be for the tool to recognize it. Larger values allow you to be less precise when tracing. Smaller values are helpful when selecting detailed areas of an image.

Note: You can increase or decrease Width settings by pressing the bracket keys as you trace with the Magnetic Lasso tool. Press] to increase and [to decrease the Width value.

The Edge Contrast option allows you to set a value for detecting the edges of an object. Lower values are better for detecting edges that are less defined; higher values are better for detecting well-defined edges. The Frequency option lets you set the rate at which the tool adds anchor points to the selection path. Higher Frequency values increase the number of anchor points added to the selection path as you trace (see Figure 2.18).

Figure 2.18 Using the Magnetic Lasso tool with a lower Frequency value (top) generates relatively few anchor points. Using a higher Frequency value (bottom) generates more anchor points.

Here are some additional tips for selecting with the Magnetic Lasso tool:

- If your selection path strays from the edge of the object, trace backward to fix it. Tracing backward will not erase anchor points.

- Press the Backspace key (Windows) or Delete key (Mac) to erase unwanted anchor points.

- Click to add anchor points manually as you trace.

- Alt-click (Windows) or Opt-click (Mac) as you trace to temporarily switch to the Polygonal Lasso tool for a straight-line segment. Click again to add an anchor point and switch back to the Magnetic Lasso.

- To close a selection path drawn with the Magnetic Lasso tool, double-click or press Enter (Windows) or Return (Mac).

When used properly, the Magnetic Lasso can be a very powerful tool for removing an object from its background, as evidenced by the yellow blossom shown in Figure 2.19. This flower is now ready to place in whatever image I choose.

Figure 2.19
A perfect Magnetic
Lasso tool selection

The Polygonal Lasso Tool

Although it's not nearly as slick as the Magnetic Lasso, the Polygonal Lasso still offers you much more control than the traditional Lasso. It is designed to select objects using nothing but straight-line segments. Because it prohibits you from selecting any curved areas, the types of objects you can select with it are severely limited. However, despite that limitation, there's still a lot you can select using the Polygonal Lasso (see Figure 2.20).

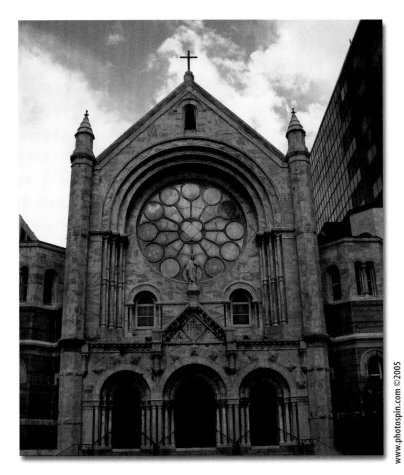

www.photospin.com ©2005

Figure 2.20 The church in this photograph is made up of nothing but straight edges, which makes the Polygonal Lasso the perfect tool for selecting it.

To access the Polygonal Lasso tool, click and hold the currently visible Lasso tool icon in the Tools palette and select Polygonal Lasso Tool from the pop-up menu that appears (see Figure 2.21). You can also toggle between the Lasso, Magnetic Lasso, and Polygonal Lasso tools by pressing L.

To make a normal selection with the Polygonal Lasso, examine the options bar to make sure Anti-alias is selected and the Feather amount is set to 0px. Click once to create a starting line segment and proceed to trace around the image. You do not need to hold the mouse button down as you trace. Each additional click creates a connecting, straight-line segment (see Figure 2.22).

Figure 2.21
The Polygonal Lasso tool

Figure 2.22 Move the mouse in the direction you'd like each line segment to follow, then click to secure it in place.

Here are some additional tips for selecting with the Polygonal Lasso tool:

- Press the Backspace key (Windows) or Delete key (Mac) to erase unwanted angles.
- Press and hold the Shift key as you draw to constrain the angle of the line segments to the nearest increment of 45°.
- To close a selection path drawn with the Polygonal Lasso tool, double-click or press Enter (Windows) or Return (Mac). You can also close the path by hovering over the start point and clicking (see Figure 2.23).

Figure 2.23
When you see the small circle appear next to the Lasso cursor, click to close the selection path.

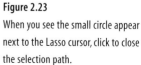

The Selection Brush

The Selection Brush allows you to make selections using brush strokes. This is a much easier and more precise way of making freeform selections than tracing with any of the lasso tools, especially if you're using a graphics pen and tablet.

The Selection Brush allows you to paint your selections using either Selection or Mask mode. The difference between these modes lies in how each one treats the selected area. Selection mode allows you to paint using a traditional marching-ants border, whereas Mask mode applies a translucent color overlay. Also, with Selection mode, the painted area becomes selected; in Mask mode, the nonpainted area becomes selected (see Figure 2.24).

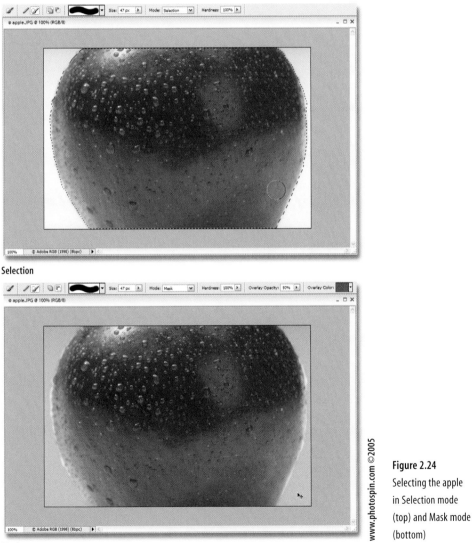

Selection

Mask

www.photospin.com ©2005

Figure 2.24
Selecting the apple in Selection mode (top) and Mask mode (bottom)

You can access the Selection Brush by pressing A on your keyboard, or by clicking and holding the currently visible selection brush icon in the Tools palette and selecting Selection Brush Tool from the pop-up menu that appears (see Figure 2.25).

Choose either Selection or Mask mode from the options bar Mode menu. With Mask mode, you can adjust the overlay opacity and choose a different overlay color. The default overlay opacity value and color is 50% red, but if these settings conflict with the photo you are working with, you can change them using the controls in the options bar.

Next, choose a brush from the preset menu in the options bar. Click the down arrow next to the brush stroke icon to reveal the preset list. You can use any brush you like for selecting, but it works best if you keep it simple. A medium-sized, hard, round pixel brush is a good one to start out with.

Adjust the brush size to cover as much area as possible with your initial strokes. Proceed to paint your selection, leaving the edges and small details for last (see Figure 2.26). As you paint, notice that the brush automatically adds to the selection any areas it comes in contact with. There is no need to hold down the Shift key.

Figure 2.25
The Selection
Brush tool

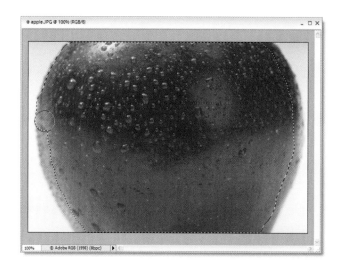

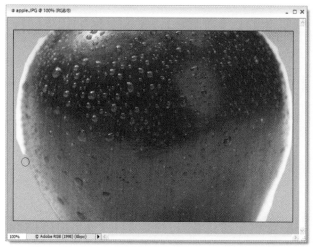

Figure 2.26
When painting with the Selection Brush in either mode, always leave the edges for last.

Tip: You can increase or decrease the brush size as you paint by pressing the bracket keys. Press] to increase and [to decrease. You can also increase/decrease the Hardness setting by pressing Shift+] or Shift+[.

Before selecting the edges, reduce the brush size accordingly. For most selections, it also helps to reduce the brush Hardness setting so that your selection edges are not too sharp. One of the benefits of painting in Mask mode is the ability to see the softness of the brush stroke. This is something that the marching ants in Selection mode can't show you (see Figure 2.27).

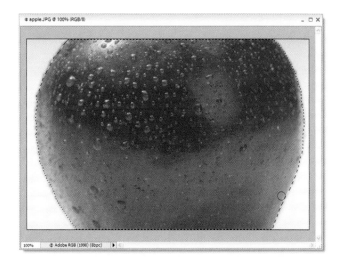

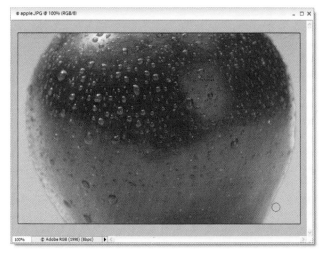

Figure 2.27
Reduce the Hardness setting and paint in the edges of the selection. In Selection mode (top), you can't see the effect of the Hardness setting, but in Mask mode (bottom), you can.

If you accidentally paint outside the edges, you can undo the last brush stroke by pressing Ctrl+Z (Windows) or ⌘+Z (Mac), or by clicking the Undo button in the shortcuts bar. You can also subtract from the selection by holding down the Alt key (Windows) or Option key (Mac) and painting over your mistake.

Painting Straight-Line Selections

To paint a straight line with the Selection Brush, click once to create a start point, then move your cursor to the end point and Shift-click. Elements automatically connects the two points.

Magic Selection Tools

Photoshop Elements also contains a series of automated "magic" selection tools. Believe it or not, these tools are designed to make selections with just one click. Once you start using them, you'll see for yourself that they truly do work like magic!

However, before you get too excited, I should warn you that there are a few stipulations. With the exception of the Magic Extractor, the magic tools are designed to select large areas of solid color. This makes them perfect for removing skies and solid color backgrounds—not busy, detailed areas of an image. Also, each magic selection tool has its own set of controls, and you need to spend some time tweaking them before you can actually make any magic happen. Nevertheless, when used with the proper settings, these tools can be huge time-savers.

The Magic Wand

The Magic Wand allows you to select large areas of color in an image with a single click. This makes it the perfect tool for selecting sky backgrounds, such as the one shown in Figure 2.28.

www.photospin.com ©2005

Before

Figure 2.28 Once I selected the blue sky in this photograph with the Magic Wand, I easily replaced it with an entirely different background image.

Continued on next page

www.photospin.com ©2005

After

Figure 2.28 *(Continued)*

Note: The accompanying CD-ROM includes a video lesson on using the Magic Wand.

To access the Magic Wand tool, press the letter W on your keyboard, or click its icon in the Tools palette (see Figure 2.29).

Before clicking in the area of the photo that you want to select, first check the options bar and make sure the proper settings are enabled. Here's a quick rundown of what each of them does:

Tolerance   If an area to be selected varies in brightness, the value entered here determines how much of the surrounding area the wand will select. The point where you click will have a specific luminosity value, and the Tolerance setting determines the range of luminosity values that will also be selected.

Anti-alias   Enabling this option softens the edges of your selection. In general, you will want to keep this option turned on at all times when making selections with any tool.

Contiguous   Enabling this option tells the Magic Wand to select adjacent regions of color. To select similar but nonadjacent regions, keep this option turned off.

Sample All Layers   When working with multilayered files, enabling this option allows you to select regions of color on all layers.

Figure 2.29
The Magic
Wand tool

Tolerance: 32   ☑ Anti-alias ☑ Contiguous ☐ Sample All Layers

The Tolerance value you should use depends on the range of luminosity values present in the colored background that you are trying to select. The wider the range of values, the higher the setting needs to be in order to make the selection with one click.

Even though the sky shown in Figure 2.28 is clearly blue, if you look closely, there are many variations of blue throughout. These variations are measured in luminosity values. By default, the Tolerance control is set to select luminosity values 32 shades lighter or darker than the initial color selected where you clicked with the wand. This means that if you click anywhere in the background with the Magic Wand, you might not select the entire sky. When this happens, you have three options:

- Undo the selection by pressing Ctrl+Z. Then raise the Tolerance value to something higher than 32 and try again (see Figure 2.30).

Figure 2.30
Top: With the Tolerance value set to 32 (the default), I was unable to select the entire sky background with just one click of the Magic Wand; the upper-right corner was too dark. Bottom: Setting the Tolerance value to 60 did the trick.

- Modify the selection using the Select > Grow or Select > Similar commands (for more on this, see Chapter 3).

- Shift-click the unselected area to add it to the selection (for more on this, see Chapter 3).

If the opposite happens, and you select more than the intended area, choose Edit > Undo, decrease the Tolerance value, and try again.

The Magic Eraser

Although it's technically not a selection tool, the Magic Eraser makes it extremely easy to isolate images from a solid color background and include them in a combined image project. The tool is designed to erase large areas of color in an image with a single click. In many instances, this makes it an even better tool than the Magic Wand for replacing backgrounds (see Figure 2.31).

To access the Magic Eraser tool, click and hold the currently visible Eraser tool icon in the Tools palette and select Magic Eraser from the pop-up menu that appears (see Figure 2.32). You can also toggle between the Eraser, Background Eraser, and Magic Eraser tools by pressing E.

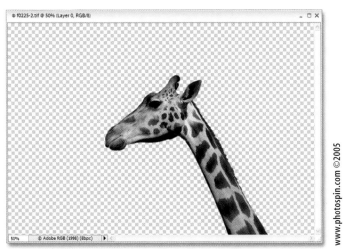

www.photospin.com ©2005

Figure 2.31
With the Magic Eraser, we can erase the sky in this image with just one click.

Note: Another way to toggle between the Eraser, Background Eraser, and Magic Eraser tools is to Alt-click (Windows) or Opt-click (Mac) the currently visible Eraser tool icon in the Tools palette.

The Magic Eraser includes the same options bar controls as the Magic Wand (described in the previous section), plus an additional Opacity setting that allows you to make a region of color translucent (instead of erasing it completely). Before clicking in the area of the photo that you want to erase, first check the options bar and make sure the proper settings are enabled.

To erase the entire sky background shown in Figure 2.31, only the Anti-aliased option needed to be selected. As with the Magic Wand tool, if you enable Tolerance, the proper value depends on the range of luminosity values present in the colored background that you are trying to erase. The wider the range of values, the higher the setting needs to be to erase the area with one click.

Figure 2.32
The Magic Eraser

Like any sky background, the one shown in Figure 2.31 contains many luminosity values. Remember, by default the Tolerance control is set to select luminosity values 32 levels lighter or darker than the initial clicking point. If you click anywhere in the background using the default Tolerance setting, you may not erase the entire sky.

When this happens you have two options:

- Undo the erasure by pressing Ctrl+Z (Windows) or ⌘+Z (Mac). Then raise the Tolerance value to something higher than 32 and try again (see Figure 2.33).
- Click in the remaining areas to erase them. You can raise or lower the Tolerance value as needed when using this method.

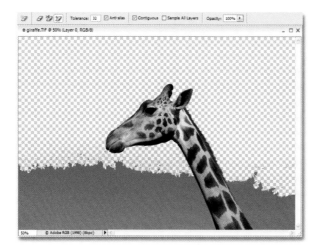

Figure 2.33a
With the Tolerance value set to 32 (the default), I was able to erase the entire sky background with just one click of the Magic Eraser.

Continued on next page

CHAPTER 2: MAKING GOOD SELECTIONS ■

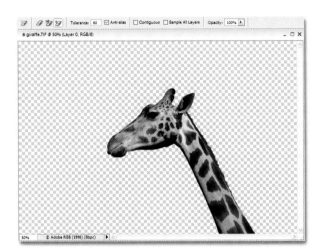

Figure 2.33b *(Continued)* Setting the Tolerance value to 60 did the trick.

The Magic Eraser also has the tendency to leave stray pixels that are difficult to see over the default transparent, gray-and-white checkerboard. To reveal any remaining artifacts, it helps if you change the default preference settings for this transparency grid. Choose Edit > Preferences > Transparency (Windows) or Photoshop Elements > Preferences > Transparency (Mac). In the dialog that appears, click the bottom-left color swatch and change it to a bright red using the Color Picker (Figure 2.34, top). Click OK to close the Color Picker and then click the right color swatch in Preferences. Proceed to change the color to a dark red (Figure 2.34, bottom). Click OK to close the Preferences dialog.

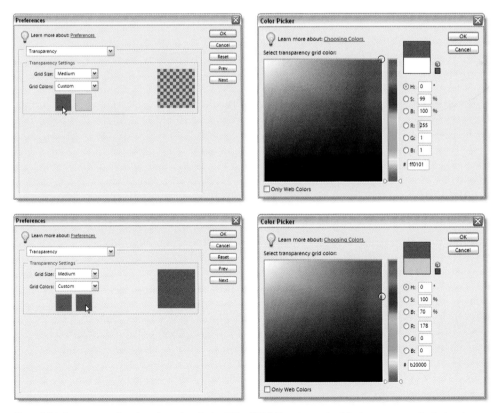

Figure 2.34 You can enter the values shown here in the RGB or HSB field to change the default transparency checkerboard colors to red.

With the transparent checkerboard color changed to red, it's much easier to see the blue artifacts left behind by the Magic Eraser (see Figure 2.35, top). To eliminate these artifacts, click the Undo icon in the shortcuts bar (or press Ctrl+Z (Windows) or ⌘+Z (Mac)), and increase the Tolerance setting. Click in the sky area again to erase it, and inspect the image for any leftover blue pixels (see Figure 2.35, bottom).

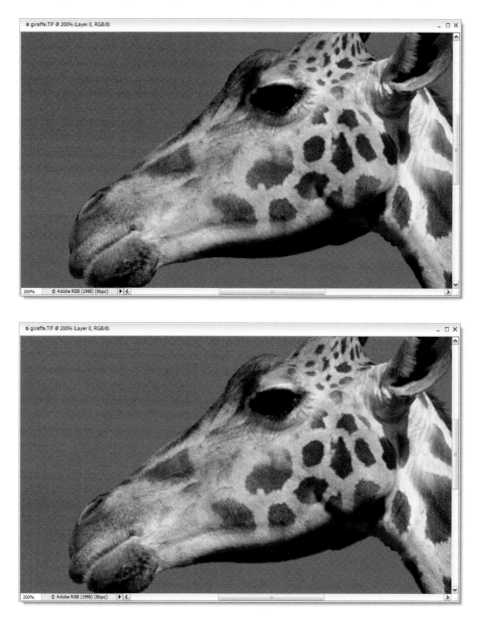

Figure 2.35 Top: Changing the checkerboard to red reveals several blue pixels along the edge that weren't erased the first time. Bottom: After clicking the Undo icon and entering a higher Tolerance setting (85 in this example), clicking once with the Magic Eraser shows us that we really did erase the entire sky this time.

It's also possible to raise the Tolerance value too high and accidentally erase pixels in the object that you're trying to isolate (see Figure 2.36). When this happens, apply the Edit > Undo command, decrease the Tolerance value, and try again.

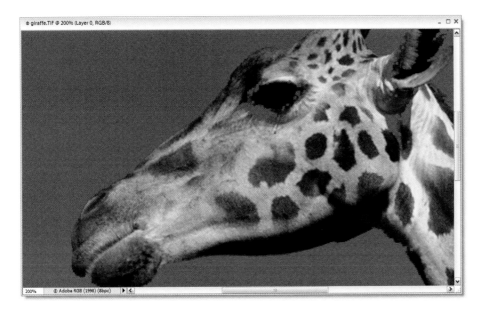

Figure 2.36 Be careful not to raise the Tolerance value too high (125 in this example), or you could wind up erasing too much of the image.

The Magic Selection Brush

With the Magic Selection Brush, Photoshop Elements takes the concept of the Selection Bush and automates it (see "The Selection Brush" section earlier in this chapter for more on the Selection Brush). The idea here is to click once on an object or draw a short brush stroke over it, and—presto! The brush magically selects the object for you.

I know, I know. This sounds a lot like the Magic Wand, and in a lot of ways it is very similar. What makes the Magic Selection Brush different is that with just one brush stroke or click, you can select a region of more than one color at a time. For example, consider our giraffe and sky again. Rather than selecting the sky background with the Magic Wand, we can instead use the Magic Selection Brush to select the forefront object, which in this case is the giraffe.

Before the Magic Selection Brush was invented, the only way to select the Giraffe shown in Figure 2.31 earlier was to trace it with one of the lasso tools or paint it with the Selection Brush. So which would you rather do? Click once on the giraffe or spend several minutes tracing it freehand?

Figure 2.37
The Magic
Selection Brush

You can access the Magic Selection Brush by pressing F on your keyboard, or by clicking and holding the currently visible selection brush icon in the Tools palette and selecting Magic Selection Brush Tool from the pop-up menu that appears (see Figure 2.37).

To give yourself more control over the automated selection, be sure to set the proper brush size in the options bar before clicking on the object. It helps if you choose a brush size that is large enough to overlap two or more colors of theobject you are trying to select (see Figure 2.38). Ultimately, it is your brush size and where you click or draw your stroke in the photograph that determines whether the Magic Brush selection is successful.

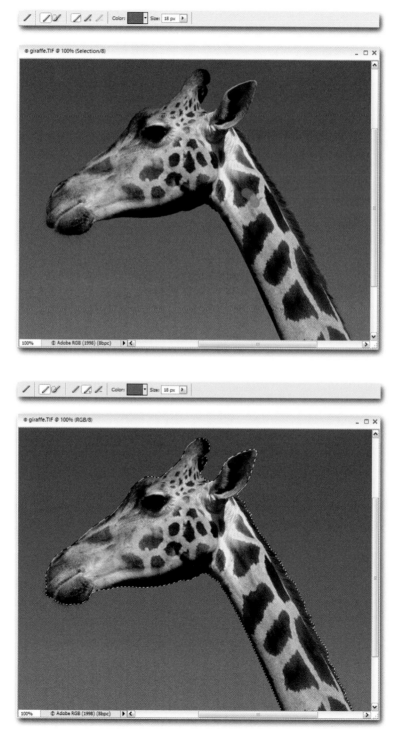

Figure 2.38
With this example, I was able to select the entire giraffe by setting the brush size to 18px and drawing a stroke over the beige color of its body and the brown color of its spots.

After generating the selection, Elements records your brush stroke and immediately switches to the Indicate Foreground tool (see Figure 2.39). If you weren't able to select the entire object with your first click or stroke, you can add to it using the Indicate Foreground tool. If the opposite happens and you wind up selecting more pixels than you had intended, you can use the Indicate Background tool to subtract them. For more on refining magic brush selections, see Chapter 3.

Figure 2.39

Magic Selection Brush options

You can also select a different color for your brush stroke in the options bar. The default color is red, but if you're trying to select a red object such as a rose, it may be too difficult to see. To make your brush stroke stand out better, click the red swatch in the options bar and choose a different color with the Color Picker.

The Magic Extractor

Although it's technically a dialog and not a tool, the Magic Extractor works like a cross between the Magic Selection Brush and the Magic Eraser. It allows you to select an object and extract it from its background with just a few clicks. This can be an extremely powerful method of isolating objects for combined image projects (see Figure 2.40).

Figure 2.40 The Magic Extractor is the perfect tool for separating detailed objects, such as this flower, from a busy background.

You can access the Magic Extractor by choosing Image > Magic Extractor. This launches a whole new interface, complete with a large preview window and its own set of tools (see Figure 2.41).

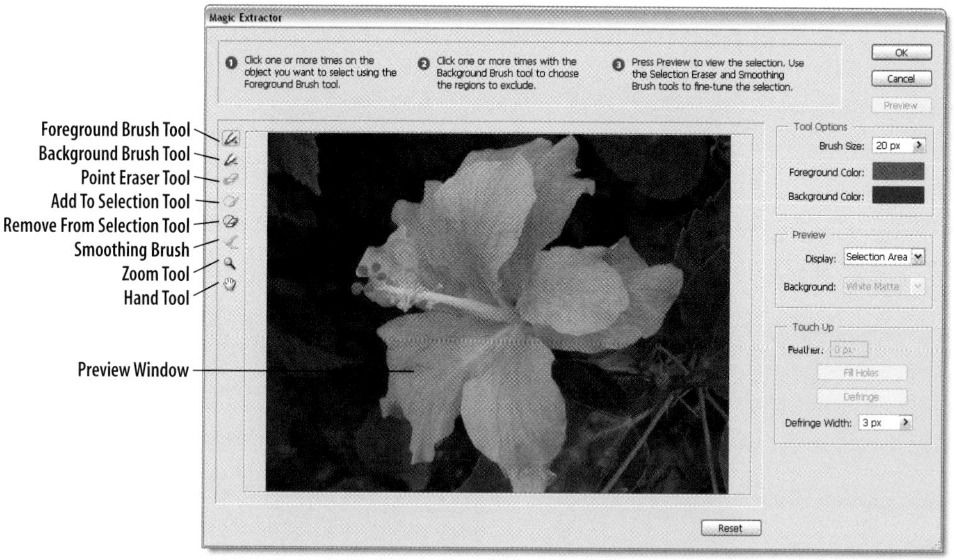
Magic Extractor
Click one or more times on the object you want to select using the Foreground Brush tool.
Click one or more times with the Background Brush tool to choose the regions to exclude.
Press Preview to view the selection. Use the Selection Eraser and Smoothing Brush tools to fine-tune the selection.
OK
Cancel
Preview
Foreground Brush Tool
Background Brush Tool
Point Eraser Tool
Add To Selection Tool
Remove From Selection Tool
Smoothing Brush
Zoom Tool
Hand Tool
Preview Window
Tool Options
Brush Size: 20 px
Foreground Color:
Background Color:
Preview
Display: Selection Area
Background: White Matte
Touch Up
Fill Holes
Defringe
Defringe Width: 3 px
Reset

Figure 2.41 The Magic Extractor interface

Note: The accompanying CD-ROM includes a video lesson on using the Magic Extractor.

When you launch the Magic Extractor, the photo you currently have open appears in the preview window. You can then indicate what the foreground and background areas are by marking different areas of the photo with the Foreground and Background Brush tools (see Figure 2.42).

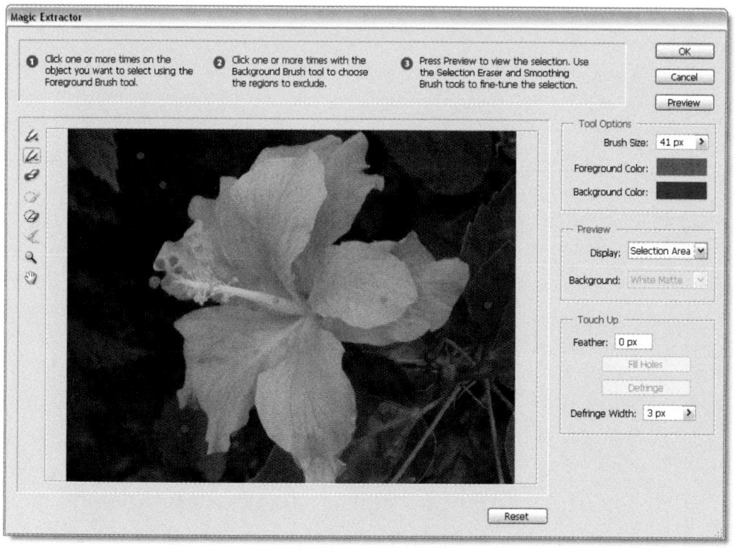
Magic Extractor
Click one or more times on the object you want to select using the Foreground Brush tool.
Click one or more times with the Background Brush tool to choose the regions to exclude.
Press Preview to view the selection. Use the Selection Eraser and Smoothing Brush tools to fine-tune the selection.
OK
Cancel
Preview
Tool Options
Brush Size: 41 px
Foreground Color:
Background Color:
Preview
Display: Selection Area
Background: White Matte
Touch Up
Feather: 0 px
Fill Holes
Defringe
Defringe Width: 3 px
Reset

Figure 2.42 Make as many marks as necessary in the preview window to indicate the intended background and foreground areas of the extraction.

Tip: To limit what appears in the dialog preview window, select an area of the photo with one of the marquee selection tools before launching the Magic Extractor.

By default the Foreground Brush color is red and the Background Brush color is blue. However, if these colors conflict with the photo you are working with, you can click the color swatches at the right of the interface and choose a different color with the Color Picker.

You can change the brush size by entering a different pixel amount in the Brush Size field located under Tool Options. You can also change the brush size by clicking the arrow next to the field and using the pop-up slider, or by pressing the left and right bracket keys.

Note: When extracting a detailed object, dragging across all of its varied colors and textures with the Foreground Brush tool ensures a more accurate selection.

As you add marks with the Foreground and Background Brushes, you can navigate around the image using the dialog's Zoom and Hand tools. If you prefer, you can use Ctrl and plus (+) or Ctrl and minus (-) (Windows) or ⌘ and plus (+) or ⌘ and minus (-) (Mac) to zoom in and out. You can also press and hold the spacebar to temporarily access the Hand tool.

When you've finished marking the foreground and background areas of the photo, click the Preview button in the upper right of the dialog to see the extraction before it is applied (see Figure 2.43). The Display menu allows you to choose whether to make the selection area or the original photo visible in the window. You can also toggle between these two display options by pressing X.

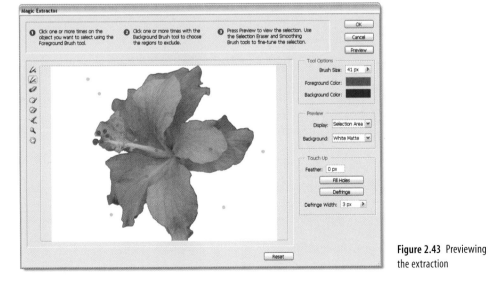

Figure 2.43 Previewing the extraction

The Background menu allows you to choose from several display options for the selection area background. The default None setting displays the selection over the current transparency display preference. Unless you've changed it (as described in "The Magic Eraser" section earlier in the chapter), this displays the default gray-and-white checkerboard pattern. Previewing over this background can make it very difficult to see any unwanted small pixel artifacts that didn't get erased. It also makes it difficult to see any unwanted fringe pixels remaining around the edges of the object. To clearly see what was erased and what wasn't as you're previewing an extracted selection, the best background color choice is White Matte (see Figure 2.44).

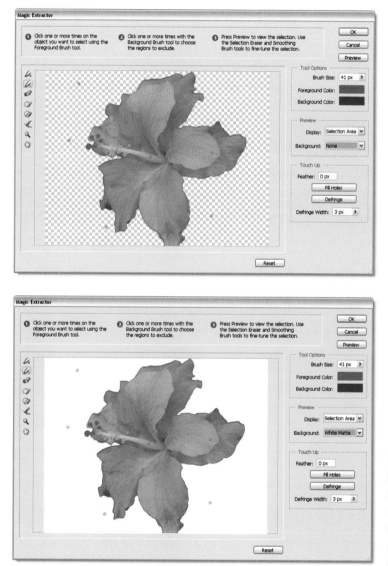

Figure 2.44 Top: With no background (the default), it's hard to see if any unwanted pixel artifacts exist. Bottom: The white matte background clearly reveals any remaining pixel artifacts and fringe colors.

Using the Magic Extractor Effectively

If necessary, you can use the various cleanup tools to fine-tune your selection and update it by clicking Preview. Here are some tips for improving your extraction:

- Add or subtract additional areas of the image by clicking or drawing with Foreground or Background Brush tools.

- Add to the selection manually by painting over specific areas with the Add To Selection tool. You can resize the brush using the same controls and key commands as when working with Foreground and Background Brush tools. To control brush softness/hardness, press the numbers 1 through 9 on your keyboard— 1 being the softest and 9 the hardest.

- Subtract from the selection manually by painting over specific areas with the Remove From Selection tool. Brush size and opacity controls work the same as with the Add To Selection tool (see above).

- Use the Point Eraser tool to remove any foreground or background marks.

- Smooth the edges of the foreground selection by painting over them with the Smoothing Brush.

- Soften the edges of the selection by increasing the pixel feather amount in the Feather box.

- Reduce fringe colors left around the edges of your selection by increasing the pixel value in the Defringe box.

- Click the Fill Holes button to seal any remaining gaps in the selection.

- Separate and remove a section from the extracted object by drawing a line through it with the Remove From Selection tool and clicking Fill Holes.

- Click the Reset button to start over.

Once your selection is complete, click OK to apply. If it's not visible already, choose Window > Layers. Notice that the object now resides on a single, transparent layer extracted from its former background. To save your extracted image without overwriting the original photo, choose Save As and name it something different.

The Background Eraser

The Background Eraser makes it easy to isolate images from a complex background. The tool is designed to evaluate the edges of an object and erase any surrounding colors. This makes it a much more powerful tool than the Magic Eraser for removing an object from its background (see Figure 2.45).

www.photospin.com ©2005

Figure 2.45 The Background Eraser is a good tool for removing this detailed flower from its busy background.

To access the Background Eraser, click and hold the currently visible Eraser tool icon in the Tools palette and select Background Eraser Tool from the pop-up menu that appears (see Figure 2.46). You can also toggle between the Eraser, Background Eraser, and Magic Eraser tools by pressing E.

Figure 2.46
The Background Eraser

The Background Eraser has its own set of controls in the options bar. Here's a quick rundown of what each of them does:

Brush Click the brush preview icon (or the down arrow directly next to it) to reveal a pop-up palette containing various brush controls, including diameter, hardness, spacing, angle, and roundness. There are also size and tolerance settings located at the bottom of the palette for working with a pressure-sensitive graphics tablet.

Limits This option tells Elements what colors to erase within the chosen brush diameter. The default Contiguous setting erases any colors within the Tolerance range that are adjacent to the sampling point (indicated by the + located in the center of the Background Eraser cursor). The Discontiguous setting allows the Background Eraser to jump over colors, occasionally into the foreground object. Therefore, Contiguous is generally the better option.

Tolerance The percentage entered here determines how close a color must be to the sampling point in order for it to be erased.

The best way to isolate an image with the Background Eraser is to choose a smaller brush size, place the sampling point just outside the edge of the object, and trace around it. The outer edge of the brush cursor circle should overlap the edge of the object as you trace (see Figure 2.47). For best results, paint slowly and use multiple brushstrokes.

Figure 2.47
A brush size of 60px s just enough to define the edge of this detailed flower.

Transparency Color Preferences

If the default gray-and-white transparency checkerboard makes it too hard to see the edge of your selection, you can change it in the Preferences dialog. Choose Edit > Preferences > Transparency (Windows) or Photoshop Elements > Preferences > Transparency (Mac). In the dialog that appears, click each color swatch to access the Color Picker. Proceed to change the default colors to something that offers better contrast with your image.

If the results are uneven, choose Window > Undo History to display the Undo History palette, and revert to the last state before the first stroke was applied. Lower the Tolerance setting and trace again. Keep testing until you find the right Tolerance setting. Although working with the Background Eraser requires a lot of trial and error, it can be an accurate way of removing a detailed selection from its background.

Once the edge is defined, you can use the Eraser tool to remove the rest of the Background (see Figure 2.48).

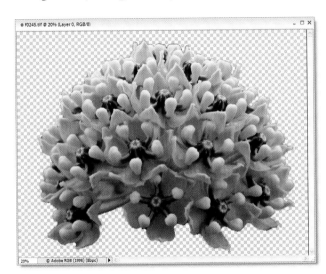

Figure 2.48
Setting the Eraser tool opacity value to 100% and the brush size to 400px allowed me to erase the remaining background area quickly and easily.

Modifying Selections

In Chapter 2 we reviewed the basic selection tools and techniques that Photoshop Elements provides, and in the examples you saw that the selections we made had to be quite simple to be done with a single tool. In many instances, it can be too difficult to select an entire object or region of a photo using just one method or tool. In fact, "good selections" are often made in steps. This involves making your initial selection and then altering it using additional tools, commands, and key modifiers. It might also require that you invert the selection path or change its edges. In this chapter we'll look at the different ways you can modify selections and how you can save them for later use in a document.

Chapter Contents

Adding and Subtracting

There are several ways to add pixels—parts of an image—to a selection or subtract them. Elements provides keystroke modifiers that allow you to add or subtract pixels when selecting with certain tools, such as the Magic Wand, the lasso tools, and the marquee tools. Menu commands are also available that enable you to expand or contract a selection path. To make things even easier, you can also add to or subtract from a selection using the Selection Brush.

Some tools, such as the Magic Selection Brush and the Magic Extractor, allow you to add or subtract pixels by choosing different tool options in the interface (see Figures 3.1 and 3.2). The Magic Selection Brush includes an Indicate Foreground and an Indicate Background option. Depending on what you are selecting in the image (foreground or background), each option lets you add pixels to a Magic Selection Brush path. Similarly, the Magic Extractor dialog includes its own set of tools, such as the Add To Selection tool and Remove From Selection tools.

Figure 3.1 The Magic Selection Brush options

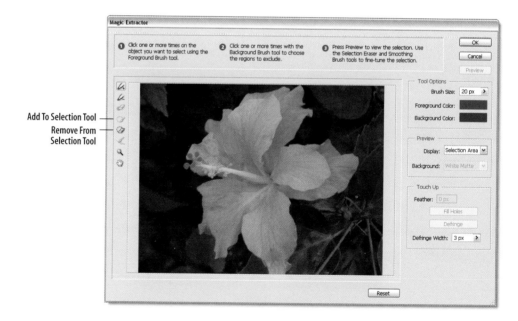

Figure 3.2 The Magic Extractor Add To Selection and Remove From Selection tools

To clear all foreground and background marks made with the Magic Selection Brush, click the New Selection icon in the options bar. To clear all foreground and background marks made in the Magic Extractor dialog, click the Reset button.

Keystroke Modifiers

The quickest and easiest way to clean up messy selections is to apply the Shift and Alt keys (Windows) or the Shift and Option keys (Mac) as you work with the selection tools. Pressing and holding Shift and Alt (Windows) or Option (Mac) as you drag or click with the tool enables you to add or subtract pixels from an existing selection path. Shift allows you to add; Alt (Windows) or Option (Mac) allows you to subtract. This can be an extremely useful way to fine-tune selection paths.

For example, you've seen that clicking once with the Magic Wand can result in an incomplete selection. If the Tolerance setting is too low, some pixels may get left behind. If it is too high, you may wind up selecting more pixels than you need. When this happens, rather than applying the Undo command (Ctrl+Z - Windows / ⌘+Z - Mac) and re-selecting, it may be easier to adjust the Tolerance level and add or subtract the desired pixels using the Shift and Alt (Windows) or Option (Mac) key modifiers (see Figure 3.3).

Figure 3.3
Hold down the Shift and Alt (Windows) or Option (Mac) keys and click with the wand in the areas you want to add or subtract.

The Shift+Alt (Windows) or Shift+Opt (Mac) key modifiers also come in handy when fine-tuning selections made with the free-form Lasso tool (Figure 3.4) or the Polygonal Lasso tool, which doesn't let you create curves (Figure 3.5).

Figure 3.4
It's hard to be accurate when tracing with the Lasso. By applying the Shift and Alt (Windows) or Option (Mac) key modifiers once a selection path is closed, you can add or subtract pixels to the selected area.

Figure 3.5
The Alt key (Windows) or Option key (Mac) modifier allows you to add curves to a closed selection path made with the Polygonal Lasso tool.

The Expand/Contract Commands

The Expand and Contract commands allow you to increase or decrease the area of an enclosed selection path such as an ellipse or rectangle. To apply the commands, all you need to do is make your initial selection, then choose Select > Modify > Expand Or Contract. In the dialog that appears, enter a pixel amount and click OK.

Adding or subtracting pixels in this way can be an extremely useful way to fine-tune selection paths made with the Rectangular or Elliptical Marquee tools. As you now know, lining the selection path up to the exact edge of an object can be rather difficult with these tools. If your path winds up too far inside or outside an object, you can use the Expand and Contract commands to add or subtract pixels around the entire selection (see Figure 3.6).

The Spacebar Modifier

When selecting with the Rectangular or Elliptical Marquee tools, you can move a selection path as you draw it by holding down the spacebar. This allows for greater precision when selecting geometric objects and can eliminate the need for modifying with the Expand and Contract commands.

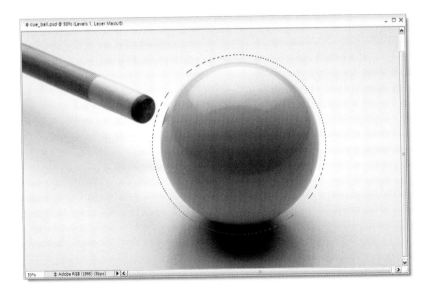

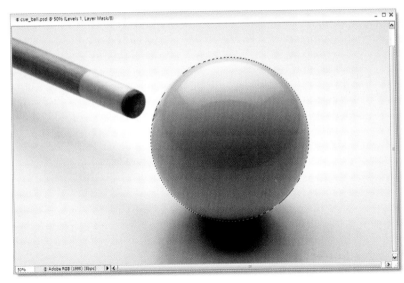

Figure 3.6 Top: This Elliptical Marquee tool selection is positioned too far away from the edge of the foreground object. Bottom: Contracting 30 pixels positions the selection path right to the edge of the object.

The Grow/Similar Commands

You can also expand an existing selection by applying either the Grow or the Similar command. These commands can be applied to any type of selection, but they are best used to expand those you've made with the Magic Wand tool. Each command adds pixels to your selection based on the current Tolerance setting.

Choose Select > Grow to add only *contiguous* (adjacent) pixels to an existing selection. To add both *contiguous* and *noncontiguous* pixels to a selection, choose Select > Similar (see Figure 3.7).

The difference between the two commands is comparable to making a Magic Wand selection with the Contiguous option turned on or off (see Chapter 2, "Making Good Selections").

For example, if you click in the sky area of the photo shown in Figure 3.7 with the Magic Wand Tolerance level set to the default 32, you wind up selecting most of the sky but not all of it. Without changing the Tolerance level, you can expand the range of the Magic Wand by applying the Grow or Similar command. If the Grow or Similar command does not complete the sky selection, try raising the Tolerance level and applying the command again.

Figure 3.7 The effect of the Grow and Similar commands. (a) The Original Magic Wand Selection. (b) the Grow command applied.

Continued on next page

Figure 3.7 *(Continued)* (c) The selection with the Similar command applied. (d) Raising the Tolerance level and applying the Grow command again completes the sky selection perfectly.

The Selection Brush

You learned how to make basic selections with the Selection Brush in Chapter 2. This tool also allows you to modify selections in the same way using brush strokes. In general, this is a much easier and more precise way of adding and subtracting pixels to a selection than working with the Lasso, especially if you're using a graphics pen and tablet.

Brushes in Elements have a natural feel to them, which makes modifying selections with the Selection Brush more comfortable than with the Lasso. To add to a selection, you just choose an appropriate brush size and paint. You do not have to hold down the Shift key modifier to add pixels; however, to subtract pixels, you must hold down the Alt key (Windows) or Option key (Mac) (see Figure 3.8).

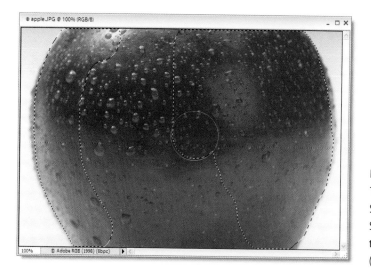

Figure 3.8
There is no need to hold down Shift when adding pixels with the Selection Brush; however, to subtract you must hold down Alt (Windows) or Option (Mac).

Changing a Selection's Edge

Another way to modify selections is to alter the edge of the selection path. Photoshop Elements contains several menu commands that allow you to make edge adjustments. These options include a Border command for converting a selection path to a soft, border-only selection; a Smooth command for simplifying detailed selections and rounding sharp corners; a Feather command for softening edges; and an Invert command for reversing the selection area.

Border

By applying the Border command to a selection, you can add a custom, soft-edged outer glow to an image. This can be a great way to add border effects to layer objects in your combined image projects. The Border command provides a more flexible way to apply outer glow effects to your image layers. Having more control over the glow effect means not having to always rely on the somewhat limiting built-in styles (for more on styles, see Chapter 8, "Adding Filters, Styles, and Effects").

To apply the Border command, select an object, such as the giraffe shown in Figure 2.31 of Chapter 2, and choose Select > Modify > Border. Enter a pixel width amount in the dialog that appears and click OK.

Once the Border command is applied, the selection path automatically takes the shape of the border width you've entered in the dialog. You can then add a new layer by choosing Layer > New > Layer or by clicking the Create A New Layer button at the top of the Layers palette. You'll want to rename the new layer "outer glow" (for the effect you'll apply to it) and position it behind the foreground object layer (see Figure 3.9).

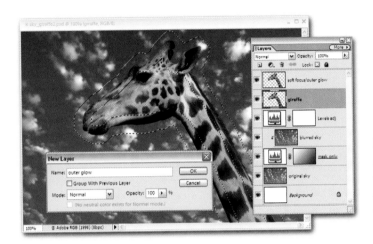

Figure 3.9
Applying a 50-pixel border selection (which expands the original outline selection 50 pixels outward from the center), and creating a new "outer glow" layer.

With the outer glow layer selected in the Layers palette, your next step is to fill the border selection with a color. If you like, you can reset the application default colors of black foreground and white background by pressing D on the keyboard (or by clicking the default colors button located at the bottom of the Tools palette), or you can choose a custom color with the Color Picker. To access the Color Picker, double-click the Foreground color icon at the bottom of the Tools palette. Proceed to choose a new color and click OK to close the dialog. To fill your selection with the new foreground color, press Alt+Backspace (Windows) or Opt+Delete (Mac) (see Figure 3.10).

Note: Alt+Backspace (Windows) or Opt+Delete (Mac) fills the current selection with the Foreground color; Ctrl+Backspace (Windows) or ⌘+Delete (Mac) fills with the Background color.

Figure 3.10
Applying a fill color of white to the border selection

Once the border is filled, you can deselect it by pressing Ctrl+D (Windows) or ⌘+D (Mac). To complete the Border command outer glow effect, lower the layer opacity level and change the layer blend mode to Screen (see Figure 3.11). For more on blend modes, see Chapter 5, "The Power of Opacity and Blending."

If you'd like to make the outer glow appear softer, you can apply a Gaussian blur effect by choosing Filter > Blur > Gaussian Blur. Enter a pixel Radius setting in the dialog and click OK. To reposition the outer glow, select the outer glow layer in the Layers palette and nudge it with the Move tool or arrow keys.

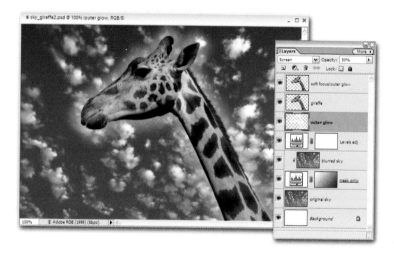

Figure 3.11
The completed Border command outer glow effect

Tip: Where did the extra layer named "soft focus/outer glow" in Figures 3.10 and 3.11 come from? It is something I applied to the image afterwards—a blurred version of the giraffe that softens the focus when the opacity level is lowered. You'll learn more about this technique in Chapter 5.

Smooth

The Smooth command does just what its name implies—it smoothes out the edges of a selection path. This can be a great way to add rounded edges to a selection made with the Polygonal Lasso tool.

For example, let's say the Polygonal Lasso is the selection tool you are most comfortable working with, and you've chosen it to select the yellow blossom shown in Figure 3.12. The only drawback to tracing with this tool is that you cannot create any curves, which there are plenty of in this image. As a result, the final selection path contains a series of sharp-edged corners rather than smooth curves (see Figure 3.12).

Figure 3.12
Selecting the yellow blossom with the Polygonal Lasso tool

To fix this, all you need to do is apply the Smooth command. With the Polygonal selection already made, choose Select > Modify > Smooth. Enter a pixel width amount in the dialog that appears and click OK.

Keep in mind that the more sharp edges there are in the selection path, the larger the sample pixel radius should be. Larger values mean smoother edges. In order to smooth the edges of the yellow blossom selection shown in Figure 3.13, I applied a 10-pixel radius.

Figure 3.13
Applying the Smooth command to this polygonal selection with a 10-pixel radius rounded the edges nicely.

Feather

By definition, a feathered edge is one that has a soft blur applied to it. You can apply these feathered edges without using the Blur filter. Feathered edges are great for creating custom glow and shadow effects, and can also be useful when blending image layers together. In Photoshop Elements, you can apply a feathered edge to a selection by pre-feathering or post-feathering.

 Note: The accompanying CD-ROM includes a video lesson on feathered selections.

Pre-feathering   When making a selection with any of the marquee or lasso tools, you can apply a feathered edge to it before it is made. These are the only selection tools that allow you to pre-feather. By entering a pixel value in the Feather field of the options bar before drawing with the tool, you are telling Elements to apply a feathered edge to the selection you are about to make. What's confusing about this is that your image won't look any different after making the selection. In order to see the soft, blurred edge, you must delete the selected area (as in Figure 3.14), make an adjustment (such as Levels or Hue And Saturation), or fill the selected area with a color.

Figure 3.14
Feathered selection edges only become apparent after deleting the selected image area, making an adjustment, or filling with a color.

 Note: Adding a feather amount in the Feather field of the options bar *after* a selection is made with the marquee or lasso tools has no effect on the current selection.

Post-feathering   To apply a feathered edge to a selection that has already been made with any selection tool, choose Select > Feather or press Alt+Ctrl+D. Enter a feather radius in the Feather Selection dialog that appears. Keep in mind that larger values result in softer edges. Click OK to close the dialog and apply the feather.

Feathering a selection after you've made it is the more common way to soften its edge, mainly because you can do it to any selection made with any tool.

In the example shown in Figure 3.15, it was possible to create a feathered mask by adding a feathered edge to the apple selection. I made the original selection with the Selection brush, and then, using the Feather command, I applied a 10-pixel feather.

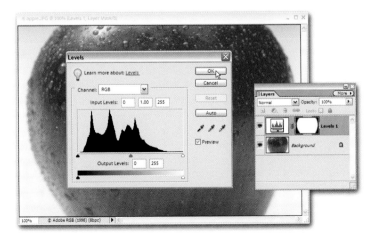

Figure 3.15
The finished Big Apple image was created using feathered layer masks.

The next step was to add a Levels adjustment layer—not to make an actual adjustment, but to gain access to its companion layer mask. Clicking OK and bypassing the Levels dialog applied a feathered mask to the image (see Figure 3.16).

Note: The Levels, Hue And Saturation, and Brightness/Contrast adjustment layers all feature a built-in layer mask, and even more important, won't affect your image if no adjustments are made. These are the adjustment layers you should use whenever your combined image project requires a layer mask but not an adjustment.

Figure 3.16
Creating a feathered layer mask

By placing the New York City photo directly above the layer mask in the Layers palette and applying the Group command (Ctrl+G - Windows / ⌘+G - Mac), I applied a feathered edge to the city photo without destroying any pixels (see Figure 3.17). This is what is called *nondestructive editing*.

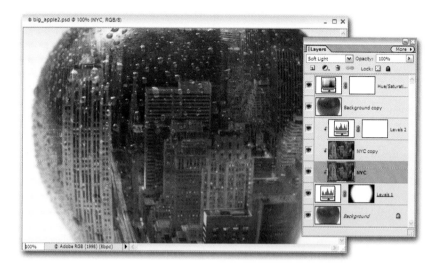

Figure 3.17 Grouping to a feathered layer mask

Note that I added the layers above the New York City layer in Figure 3.16 to enhance image detail and color. For more on this, see Chapter 4, "Mastering Layers," and Chapter 5, "The Power of Opacity and Blending."

Invert

Sometimes when you're attempting to select a detailed object, it can be easier to select the object's background first and then *invert* the selection path. Although this may sound like a backwards way to work (and it is), it can get you the end result you're looking for—and that's all that matters.

For example, in order to select the detailed apple shown in Figure 3.18, it makes more sense to select the surrounding white background area with the Magic Wand tool and *invert* the selection. The water droplets on the apple make it too difficult to select with the Magic Wand, even at a higher Tolerance setting. But by raising the Tolerance level to 50, clicking on the left side of the apple, then Shift-clicking the right side—you can select the entire background in a matter of seconds.

With the background area selected, choosing Select > Inverse, or pressing Shift+Ctrl+I (Windows) or Shift+⌘+I (Mac), reverses the selection and—presto! The detailed foreground object is now selected (see Figure 3.19).

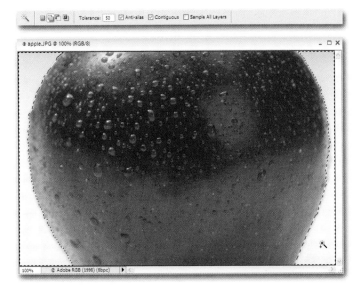

Figure 3.18
Selecting the background with the Magic Wand tool is easier than trying to select the apple.

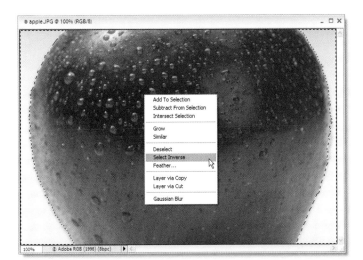

Figure 3.19
The easiest way to select the apple is to invert the background selection.

Saving and Loading Selections

With Photoshop Elements, you can also save and load your selections. This can be especially useful when making detailed selections that you might want to use again.

In Adobe Photoshop CS2 (Elements' big brother application), you can save a selection as an alpha channel or as a path. Unfortunately, in Elements there are no channels or paths. However, you can save multiple selections in a document using the Save Selection command.

If your compositing project requires that you make a complicated selection, it's always a good idea to save it just in case you need to use it again. For example, in the image shown in Figure 3.20, it was necessary to select the background area in order to mask an image inside of it. This was a tedious task, to say the least. Just to be safe, it made sense to save the selection as soon as it was completed.

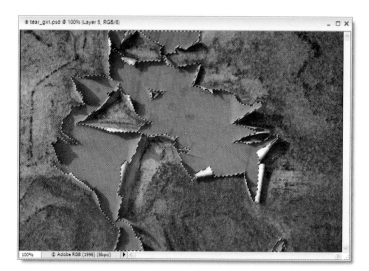

Figure 3.20
It's always a good idea to save detailed selections like the one shown here.

You wouldn't want to go through the whole tedious selection process again should you accidentally make a mistake with your project down the road. Better to avoid extra work and choose Select > Save Selection. In the dialog that appears, enter a name for the selection and click OK.

Then, any time you want to load a saved selection, choose Select > Load Selection. Choose the selection from the menu in the Load Selection dialog and click OK. Elements displays the selection path exactly as you saved it.

You can store multiple selections in a document this way and access them at any time. Also, if you open the dialog with a selection already made, you can gain access to additional options that allow you to use the Add To, Subtract From, or Intersect features with the selection that you chose from the menu.

Note: You also have the option to invert a selection as you load it. In the Load Selection dialog, choose the saved selection from the menu, click the Invert option, and click OK.

Overall, the ability to save and load detailed selections can make complicated projects like the one shown in Figure 3.21 a lot easier to manage.

Figure 3.21
The ability to save and load selections of the background and shadow areas made completing this project much easier.

Mastering Layers

Along with making good selections, mastering the use of layers is crucial to success when creating a photomontage, collage, or composite image with Photoshop Elements. What makes layers so powerful is that they allow you to sample your ideas and bring them to life. Because each layer represents only one aspect of information in your project, this means you can edit, move, blend, fine-tune, and transform each element of your composition separately before combining them. Each layer is entirely independent from the rest of the image, which leaves you lots of room for creativity and experimentation.

Like the selection techniques covered in Chapters 2 and 3, the layering skills you'll learn here will be put to use in almost every compositing project you try in Photoshop Elements.

4

Chapter Contents
Defining Layer Types
Layer Control
Adding Image Layers
Adding Effect Layers
Managing Layers

Defining Layer Types

All combined image projects created in Photoshop Elements consist of multiple layers of information. As you build your image, you can add two types of layers: image layers and what I'll describe for this discussion as *effect* layers.

Image Layers

Image layers in Elements contain either pixel- or vector-based information. Shape and type layers are vector based, while all others are pixel based. As you know from reading Chapter 1, "It All Starts with an Idea," all photographic images in Elements are made up of tiny, square pixels. Vector images are much more flexible, because they are based on mathematical curves and not pixels. Unlike pixel-based (or *raster*) layers, vector image layers can be scaled to any size.

Shape and type layers appear differently in the Layers palette. Shape layers display a vector mask containing an outline of the shape over a gray background. Type layers display a capital T to indicate that the type is editable and can also be resized (see Figure 4.1).

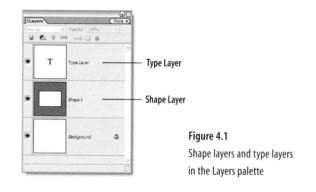

Type Layer

Shape Layer

Figure 4.1
Shape layers and type layers
in the Layers palette

The Simplify Layer Command

You can convert vector-based shape and type layers into pixel-based (raster) layers by selecting them from the Layers palette and choosing Layer > Simplify Layer. You can also right-click to access the Simplify Layer command from a selected layer's context menu.

Both raster and vector image layers can be repositioned in the Layers palette. You can also adjust their opacity level, control their visibility, change blend modes, lock/unlock, and link them to other layers.

Filters and effects cannot be applied to vector-based shape and type layers. To do so, you must convert them to pixel-based layers by applying the Simplify Layer command.

Effect Layers

Layers that allow you to apply fill overlays and tonal adjustments without permanently altering any pixels can be described as *effect* layers (although Adobe doesn't use that term). You can add two types of effect layers to your layered compositions in Photoshop Elements: Fill layers and Adjustment layers.

Both fill and adjustment layers affect all layers below them in the Layers palette. A fill layer allows you to apply a solid color, gradient, or pattern overlay to an image without permanently altering any of its pixels. An adjustment layer allows you to make nondestructive tonal adjustments to an image. You can apply the following types of adjustment layers: Levels, Brightness/Contrast, Hue/Saturation, Photo Filter, Gradient Map, Invert, Threshold, and Posterize.

> **Note:** With effect layers, you can edit images nondestructively without adding much to the overall file size of a document.

Every effect layer contains its own set of controls that is displayed immediately after adding it to the document. You can access these controls at any time by choosing Layer > Layer Content Options or by double-clicking the layer thumbnail in the Layers palette.

By default, effect layers also contain a companion layer mask. The built-in layer mask can be especially useful when combining images. Layer masks hide all or part of a layer. Anywhere the layer mask is black, the layer will be hidden. Where it is white, the layer will be revealed. Shades of gray partially hide the contents of the layer. This means that you can blend image layers together manually by painting in a layer mask with the Brush tool, or by filling selections in the mask with a color or gradient.

In addition, you can use layer masks to group image layers. In several examples throughout this book, we create a Levels, Brightness/Contrast, or Hue/Saturation adjustment layer solely for the use of its companion layer mask. You can achieve this by adding one of these three effect layers and making no adjustments at all. To apply the mask, simply apply the Group command to any images positioned directly above the effect layer in the palette (see Figure 4.2).

To Mask or Not to Mask?

If you'd prefer not to include layer masks with added adjustment layers, you can disable this automatic feature in the Palette Options dialog. To display the dialog, choose Palette Options from the Layers palette menu. Then, at the bottom of the palette, deselect the option Use Default Masks On Adjustments and click OK. With this option disabled, any new adjustment layers added to your documents will not contain a layer mask. Keep in mind, however, that layer masks do not add to your overall file size, and can be deleted independently from adjustment layers. You may want to consider leaving the default layer mask option enabled and instead deleting only any unused layer masks.

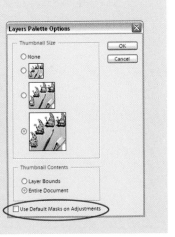

Figure 4.2 Layer masks in action

Except for their built-in controls and layer masks, effect layers contain the same opacity, visibility, blending, and grouping properties as image layers. They can also be locked, linked, and repositioned in the same way.

Layer Control

Some layer controls are located under the Layer menu, including the arrange set of commands, Duplicate Layer, and Delete Layer , but the best way to manage layers is through the Layers palette. The Layers palette contains everything you need to manage your layers. All of the controls located under the Layers menu, as well as some palette specific options (such as linking and locking), are accessible directly from the palette (see Figure 4.3).

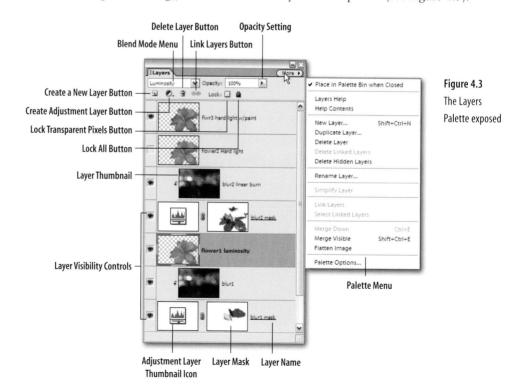

Figure 4.3

The Layers
Palette exposed

"Seeing Into" Your Image

The Layers palette gives you the power to "see into" your image. By laying out all of the pieces of your layered composition in front of you, this tool allows you to alter the way images interact by changing the layer order, applying different blend modes, and adjusting opacity settings. It also enables you to apply the same transformation to multiple layers by selecting them or linking them together. The Layers palette also offers the ability to control layer visibility, to lock and unlock layer and transparency properties, and to merge and flatten layers. To learn more about working with the Layers palette, see the video 04_01_selecting_layers.mov on the companion CD.

Controlling Layer Visibility

Even though you can "see inside" your layered document, Photoshop Elements sees layers from the top down. You can create a composite image by stacking layers on top of each other and controlling the way they interact.

One way to do this is by controlling layer visibility. The Layers palette contains visibility controls that allow you to show and hide individual layers. This can be extremely useful when you're trying out different ideas in a combined image project.

Each visible layer displays an eye icon to the left of its thumbnail in the palette. You can show or hide individual layers by clicking the eye icons (see Figure 4.4).

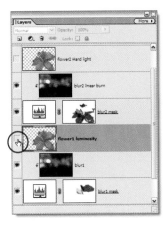

Figure 4.4
You can toggle layer visibility by clicking the eye icons in the Layers palette.

Note: You can display a single layer and hide all others by Alt-clicking (Windows) or Option-clicking (Mac) the layer's eye icon.

Think of the Layers palette as your own personal storage chest of ideas. Toggling layer visibility can help you decide which images you'd like to use in a layered composition. Add as many image layers as you like and show/hide them along the way as you're building your project. If you're not sure whether you'd like to use a specific image layer, you can always turn off its visibility and keep it stored in the document. This way, you can come back to it later when your project is further developed.

Selecting Multiple Layers

In previous versions of Photoshop Elements, you were unable to select multiple layers. But now in Elements 4 you can select contiguous layers by Shift-clicking, and non-contiguous layers by Ctrl-clicking (Windows) or ⌘-clicking (Mac) (see Figure 4.5).

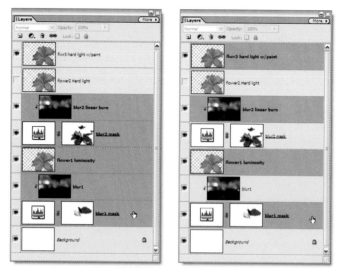

Figure 4.5
Left: Shift-clicking lets you select contiguous layers. Right: Ctrl-clicking (Windows) or ⌘-clicking (Mac) lets you select noncontiguous layers.

Shift- or Ctrl / ⌘-clicking allows you to move, reposition, transform, lock, arrange, duplicate, merge, delete, and apply styles to multiple layers at once (see Figure 4.6). To work with multiple layers in previous versions of Elements, you had to link layers together.

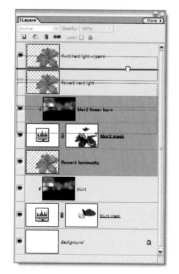

Figure 4.6
You can reposition multiple layers at once by selecting them first.

To streamline working with the Move tool, you can apply the Auto Select Layer feature in the options bar. With this option enabled, you can automatically select layers with the Move tool by pointing and clicking. All you need to do is place the tool cursor over the image you'd like to move and Elements automatically selects the layer for you. Shift-clicking other images in the document adds layers to the currently selected layer. To deselect a layer, Shift-click the image in the document.

With the Auto Select Layer option enabled and no layers selected, you can Shift-click and drag to marquee over the images whose layers you'd like to select (see Figure 4.7). When you release the mouse button, Elements automatically selects the layers containing the images you marqueed over in the document window.

Figure 4.7
Marqueeing with the Auto Select Layer option enabled

To override the enabled Auto Select Layer option, press Ctrl (Windows) or ⌘ (Mac) and click with the Move tool. This allows you to move the object on the currently selected layer, regardless of where the Move tool is positioned in the document window. If you prefer to work with the Auto Select Layer option turned off, you can temporarily enable it by Ctrl-clicking (Windows) or ⌘-clicking (Mac) with the Move tool.

Note: The check box in the options bar will not indicate when Auto Select Layer has been toggled on or off using the Ctrl key (Windows) or ⌘ key (Mac).

Photoshop Elements 4 also contains three new commands under the Select menu: All Layers, Deselect Layers, and Similar Layers.

All Layers   Selects all layers in the document. This can be especially useful when you're creating a merged version of all the layers in your composition by pressing Alt and applying the Merge Layers command. Note that the All Layers command does not recognize the Background layer.

Deselect Layers   Deselects all layers in the document. You should always deselect layers before making a Move tool marquee selection with the Auto Select Layer option enabled. Note that most of the tools and other menu commands in Elements require that at least one layer be selected.

Similar Layers   Lets you select layers based on the contents of the currently selected layer; for example, if you choose Similar Layers when a Type layer is selected, any other Type layers will also be selected. You cannot apply this command when multiple layers are selected or when the Background layer is selected. The Similar Layers command distinguishes between the following layer types: pixel-based image layers, fill layers, adjustment layers, type layers, and shape layers. Applying this command can be especially useful when making global type formatting changes, or when copy and pasting layer style settings.

Linking and Unlinking

Now that you can select multiple layers to work with in a document, the need for linking and unlinking is not as essential as in earlier versions of Elements. As a result, the Link Layers button has now replaced the former link column in the Layers palette.

Unfortunately, you cannot create layer groups in Elements, as you can in its big brother application, Photoshop CS2. Layer groups in Photoshop CS2 allow you to place multiple layers in a folder and apply opacity adjustments, blend modes, and even layer masks to the entire group. The layers remain as part of the group until they are removed from the folder. Unfortunately, this feature is not available yet in Elements; therefore, linking layers together is the only other way to "group" them. Keep in mind, however, that linking layers in Elements does not allow you to apply opacity adjustments, blend modes, or layer masks to the entire linked group as it does with layer groups in Photoshop. It does allow you to keep layers together in an orderly fashion and move or transform them.

To create a linked group, select the layers you'd like to include and click the Link Layers button at the top of the Layers palette, or choose Link Layers from the palette menu (see Figure 4.8). Provided that the selected layers are not already linked to any other layers, they all become linked.

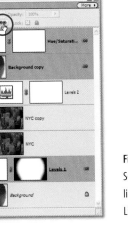

Figure 4.8
Select the layers you'd like to link and click the Link Layers button.

Linking from Mixed Selections

- You can add an unlinked layer to an existing linked set by selecting it along with at least one layer from the set, and then clicking the Link Layers button.

- If you select one or more layers from multiple linked sets and at least one unlinked layer, applying the link command creates a new linked set containing all of the selected layers. Keep in mind that when applying the link command to a mixed selection, any unselected layers that are part of the linked sets will not be included in the new linked set.

- If your selection includes a mixture of linked and unlinked layers, pressing Ctrl (Windows) or ⌘ (Mac) and clicking the Link Layers button unlinks all the layers.

To unlink all layers in a linked set, select all the layers included in the set and click the Link Layers button. To remove individual layers from a linked set, select them and click the Link Layers button.

Note: Clicking the Link Layers button with a selection containing layers from mixed link sets causes the layers to become unlinked.

You can also temporarily unlink a layer in order to apply changes to it without affecting the other layers in the linked set. To do so, press Shift and click the link icon that appears on the right side of the layer (see Figure 4.9). Elements lets you know that the link is temporarily disabled by placing a red X over the icon. Shift-click the link icon again to reenable the link.

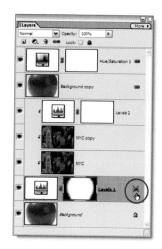

Figure 4.9

Shift-click the link icon next to the layer name to temporarily unlink the layer.

Locking and Unlocking

In Photoshop Elements, you can lock a layer's transparency only or lock all of its layer properties. Locking a selected layer's properties in the Layers palette secures its position in the document and prevents any changes from being made to it. Locking transparency restricts changes to the visible pixel area, preventing any changes from affecting the transparent areas of the layer.

To lock all layer properties, select a layer and click the Lock All button at the top of the Layers palette. Once you do, Elements displays a black lock icon on the far right of the layer in the palette (see Figure 4.10). To unlock the layer properties, select it and click the Lock All button again.

To lock only layer transparency, select a transparent layer and click the Lock Transparent Pixels button at the top of the Layers palette. By doing so, you are telling Elements to apply changes only to areas containing visible pixels (see Figure 4.11).

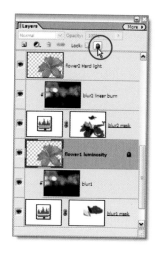

Figure 4.10

Click the Lock All button to lock all properties for the selected layer.

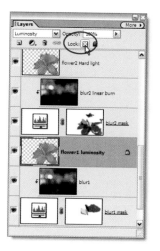

Figure 4.11

Click the Lock Transparent Pixels button to lock transparency for the selected layer.

This is a useful way to maintain the edge quality of an image when applying a Gaussian blur effect, or to keep the transparent areas of the layer clean when painting. For example, to add to the redness of the flower shown in Figure 4.12, you can paint a sampled red over the areas you'd like to enhance with a soft brush set at a low opacity, as I've done on the top. By first locking layer transparency, as I've done on the bottom, you can ensure that none of the red color will spill over into the transparent areas surrounding the flower as you paint.

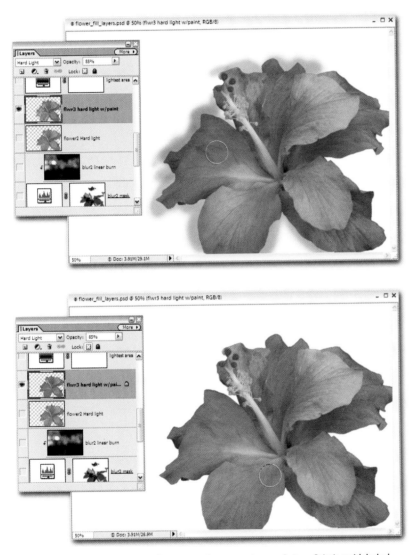

Figure 4.12 Top: Painting on a normal transparent layer can get messy. Bottom: Painting with locked transparency keeps the layer nice and clean.

To unlock layer transparency, select the locked transparent layer and click the Lock Transparent Pixels button again.

Note: Whether locking transparency or locking all layer properties, you can only lock or unlock one selected layer at a time.

Adding Image Layers

Compositing in Photoshop Elements is a process that involves adding image layers to a document, stacking them on top of each other, and using the Layers palette to control the way they interact. To start this process, you must first open the images you'd like to include in your project, and then copy them into your layered document.

The easiest way to add an image to a layered composition is to drag and drop with the Move tool. All you need to do is position the files side by side in the canvas, and then click and drag the additional image into the layered file (see Figure 4.13).

Note: Holding down Shift as you drag and drop with the Move tool centers the copied image.

Figure 4.13
You can add images by dragging and dropping with the Move tool.

It's also possible to select multiple layers at a time and drag and drop them with the Move tool into another layered document (see Figure 4.14). Any layers added to a document using the drag-and-drop method are placed above the currently selected layer in the document. If multiple layers are selected, the new layer is placed above the topmost selected layer.

You can also add images by making selections and applying the copy/paste commands. To use this method, make a selection with any of the selection tools and choose Edit > Copy. Then, in your layered document, choose Edit > Paste. Doing so places the image on its own layer above the layer that is currently selected in the palette (see Figure 4.15). If multiple layers are selected, the image is placed above the topmost selected layer. The pasted layer is automatically centered in the document and is given a default name (e.g., Layer 1).

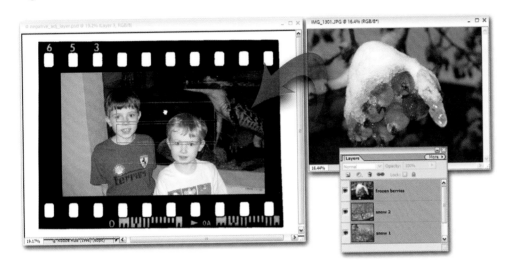

Figure 4.14 You can drag and drop multiple layers at once. Here you see the three layers highlighted in the palette appearing as outlines as they are dragged into the document on the left.

Note: Don't rely on the default layer names if you want to keep track of your compositing project. Instead, give each layer a meaningful name as it's created; the upcoming section "Naming Layers" shows how.

Figure 4.15
When you copy and paste a selected image, Elements creates a new layer above the topmost selected layer.

Creating New Layers

To create a new layer, choose Layer > New > Layer, or click the New Layer icon at the top of the Layers palette. Choosing Layer > New > Layer displays the New Layer dialog. In this dialog, you can name the new layer and choose a blending mode and opacity setting before it is created. Click OK to add a new blank layer directly above the currently selected layer in the palette. If multiple layers are selected, the new layer is placed above the topmost selected layer. You can then add content to the layer by painting with any of the available brushes, or by making a selection and filling it with a color, gradient, or pattern (see Figure 4.16).

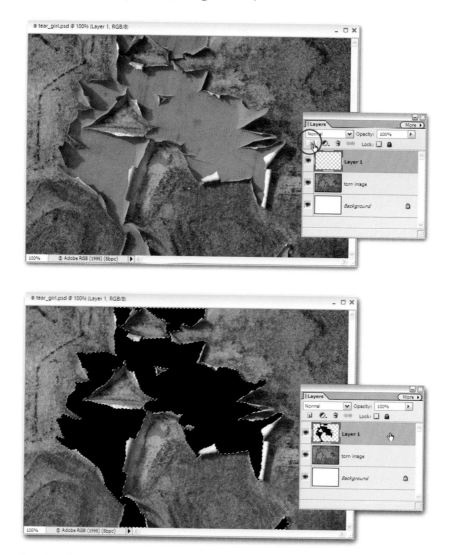

Figure 4.16 Top: Click the Create A New Layer button to add a blank layer above the topmost selected layer in the document. Bottom: One way to add content to a new layer is by making a selection and filling it.

Note: Holding down the Alt key (Windows) or Option key (Mac) when clicking the Create A New Layer button in the Layers palette displays the New Layer dialog.

You can also create new layers based on selections. This involves making a selection and duplicating or "cutting" it to a new layer directly above the currently selected layer. To duplicate, make a selection with any of the selection tools and press Ctrl+J (Windows) or ⌘+J (Mac) (see Figure 4.17). To "cut," or remove the image from the selected layer and paste it to a new layer, make a selection and press Shift+Ctrl+J (Windows) or Shift+⌘+J (Mac) (see Figure 4.18).

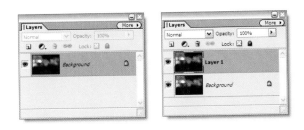

Figure 4.17
Ctrl+J (Windows) or ⌘+J (Mac) duplicates the selection and places it on a new layer.

Figure 4.18
Shift+Ctrl+J (Windows) or Shift+⌘+J (Mac) removes the image from the selected layer and places it on a new layer.

Duplicating a layer can be useful when you're experimenting with different blend modes (see Chapter 5, "The Power of Opacity and Blending"). To do so, select the layer and choose Duplicate Layer. This option can be found on the palette menu, the Layer menu, or the selected layer's context menu (accessible by right-clicking (Windows) or Control-clicking (Mac), or you can press Ctrl+J (Windows) or ⌘+J (Mac). Elements positions the duplicated layer directly above the currently selected layer in the palette with the word "copy" added to its name (unless you are duplicating the Background layer, in which case the default Layer X name is applied). If multiple layers are selected, the new layer is placed above the topmost selected layer.

To duplicate multiple layers, select them in the Layers palette and apply the Duplicate Layer command. The copied layers are all placed in a stack, directly above the topmost selected layer.

Note: The keyboard shortcut for duplicating (Ctrl+J - Windows / ⌘+J - Mac) does not work when attempting to duplicate multiple layers at once.

Naming Layers

The more layers you add to a document, the harder it becomes to keep track of them. This is why you should always name your layers appropriately as you go about building your project. Keeping things organized in the Layers palette is without a doubt the best way to manage your layers.

When you choose Layer > New > Layer, Elements displays the New Layer dialog. You can enter a name for the new layer here.

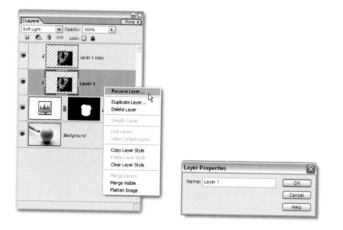

Note that clicking the Create A New Layer button does not display the New Layer dialog, and as a result the new layer is automatically given the default name Layer 1, or Layer 2, Layer 3, etc., depending on how many layers you've created this way. To access the New Layer dialog when creating new layers with the palette button, hold down the Alt key (Windows) or Option key (Mac) as you click.

If you'd like to change the name of an existing layer in the palette, you can do so by selecting the layer and choosing Rename Layer from the palette menu, the Layer menu, or the context menu displayed by right-clicking the selected layer. Choosing Rename Layer displays the Layer Properties dialog. To rename the layer, enter a new name in the field and click OK to apply.

Another, even easier way to rename a layer is by double-clicking its existing name in the palette. Doing so highlights the existing name and allows you to type in something else (see Figure 4.19).

Figure 4.19

Double-click to highlight the existing name (left) and then type in a name that better describes the layer's purpose in your project (right).

Note: Photoshop Elements does not allow you to rename multiple layers at a time. You must rename them individually.

Layer Navigation

You can reposition the order of layers in the layer stack by selecting a layer (or multiple layers), holding down the mouse button, and dragging up or down in the Layers palette. As you drag up or down, a thick black line appears between layers to indicate your current position in the layer stack. Releasing the mouse button places the layers in their new position (see Figure 4.20).

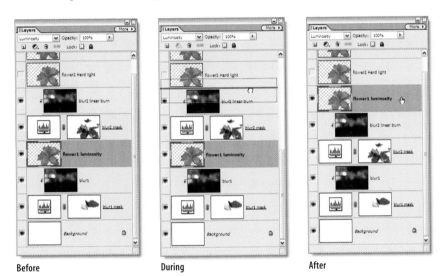

Before   During   After

Figure 4.20 To reposition a layer in the layer stack, select it, click and drag up or down, then release the mouse button.

You can use a series of keyboard shortcuts to navigate through the layer stack and reposition layers, as shown in Table 4.1.

Table 4.1 Keyboard Shortcuts for Layer Navigation

Action	Keyboard Shortcut
Activate Layer Above	Alt+] (Windows) Opt+] (Mac)
Activate Layer Below	Alt+[(Windows) Opt+[(Mac)
Move Layer Up One Position	Ctrl+] (Windows) ⌘+] (Mac)
Move Layer Down One Position	Ctrl+[(Windows) ⌘+[(Mac)
Move Layer to Top of Stack	Ctrl+Shift+] (Windows) ⌘+Shift+] (Mac)
Move Layer to Bottom of Stack	Ctrl+Shift+[(Windows) ⌘+Shift+[(Mac)
Create New Layer Below	Ctrl-click Create A New Layer button (Windows) ⌘-click Create A New Layer button (Mac)

What About the Background Layer?

As a general rule, you should never work on the Background layer. If you're starting out with a flat-tened image, you should always duplicate the Background layer before editing. You can do so by pressing Ctrl+J (Windows) or ⌘+J (Mac). If you need to, you can always hide the original Back-ground layer as you work with the layers above it in the stack. Even though it adds a bit to your file size, this is a safe, nondestructive way of working.

Adding Effect Layers

Effect layers change all layers below them in the Layers palette. By adding effect layers to your layered composition, you can apply fill overlays and tonal adjustments to your image without permanently altering any pixels. There are two different types of effect layers that you can add: fill layers and adjustment layers.

Note: To learn more about inserting effect layers, see the video 04_02_adjustment_layers.mov on the companion CD.

Adding Fill Layers

Fill layers allow you to apply a solid color, gradient, or pattern overlay to an image. To add a fill layer, choose Layer > New Fill Layer > Solid Color, Gradient, or Pattern. You can also add a fill layer by clicking the Create Adjustment Layer button at the top of the Layers palette and selecting the type of fill layer you want from the pull-down menu (see Figure 4.21).

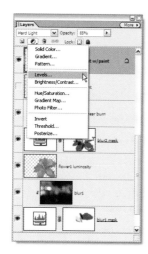

Figure 4.21

Click the Create Adjustment Layer button at the top of the Layers palette to access the pull-down menu.

Note: By holding down Alt (Windows) or Option (Mac) as you choose a fill layer option from the Create Adjustment Layer pull-down menu, you can access the New Layer dialog. This dialog allows you to name the fill layer, apply a different blend mode, change the opacity setting, and even group the new layer to the layer below—all before the layer is even added to the stack.

Here is a brief overview of the different types of Fill Layers that are available in Photoshop Elements and how you can use them in your projects:

Solid color fill layers   Including these fill layers can be a great way to apply a color tint to an image. When you add a solid color layer, Elements automatically launches the Color Picker (the same tool we used in Chapter 2 to tweak the Transparency Grid for working with the Magic Eraser; see Figure 2.28). Using this dialog, choose a fill color and click OK to apply it. If you decide to change it later, you can, because fill layers are nondestructive. Double-click the Solid Color thumbnail icon in the Layers palette to access the Color Picker again. To take your exploration one step further, try lowering the fill layer's opacity setting and experimenting with the various blend modes. Doing so can help you create solid color effects, such as a sepia tone (see Figure 4.22).

Figure 4.22 You can create a sepia tone by adding a brown solid color fill layer at the top of the layer stack and setting its blend mode to Hue.

Gradient fill layers   These can be especially useful for lightening or darkening specific areas of an image. When you add a gradient fill layer, Elements automatically launches the Gradient Fill dialog, which allows you to choose a gradient to apply, as well as several other options, including Style, Angle, and Scale. You can change these settings at any time without permanently altering any pixels. To do so, double-click the Gradient layer thumbnail icon in the Layers palette to display the Gradient Fill dialog again, make your changes, and click OK. Note also that by adjusting the gradient fill layer's opacity and blend mode settings, you can gain much greater control over your image adjustments (see Figure 4.23).

Before

After

Figure 4.23 You can add a highlight to an image by adding a custom white-to-transparent gradient fill layer and setting its blend mode to Soft Light.

Pattern fill layers   These can be used to add textures to your combined image projects. When you're adding a pattern fill layer, Elements automatically launches the Pattern Fill dialog. This dialog allows you to choose a pattern to apply, and also lets you scale the texture. You can reposition the pattern by clicking and dragging in the document window. To reset the pattern to its original position, click the Snap To Origin button.

To prevent the pattern from being moved once the Pattern Fill dialog is closed, deselect the Link With Layer option. These settings can be changed at any time without permanently altering any pixels. To change settings, double-click the Pattern layer thumbnail icon in the Layers palette to redisplay the Gradient Fill dialog (see Figure 4.24).

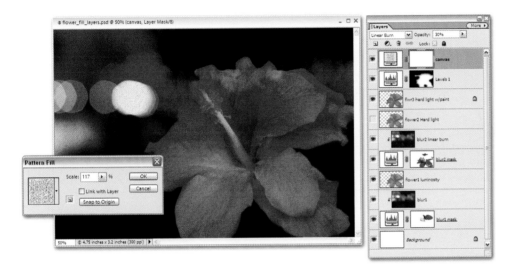

Figure 4.24 You can apply a canvas texture to an image by adding a pattern fill layer, setting its blend mode to Linear Burn, and lowering its opacity value.

Adding Adjustment Layers

Adjustment layers allow you to make nondestructive tonal and color adjustments to an image. To add an adjustment layer, choose Layer > New Adjustment Layer, or click the Create Adjustment Layer button at the top of the Layers palette and select a type of adjustment layer to add from the pull-down menu (shown earlier, in Figure 4.21). You can apply the following types of adjustment layers to a document: Levels, Brightness/Contrast, Hue/Saturation, Photo Filter, Gradient Map, Invert, Threshold, and Posterize.

Levels This type of adjustment layer allows you to make nondestructive tonal (luminosity) adjustments using the Levels dialog. When you add a Levels adjustment layer, Elements automatically launches the Levels dialog. This dialog allows you to adjust the shadow, midtone, and highlight information of an image by moving the sliders under the histogram, or by clicking with the Eyedroppers to sample locations in the image to set as its black point, white point, and neutral gray values. The black point is considered the darkest area of an image; the white point is considered the lightest area; neutral is 50% gray.

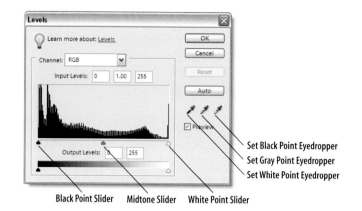

Black Point Slider   Midtone Slider   White Point Slider

Image tonality can change drastically as you add layers to a project. With Levels adjustment layers, you can fine-tune individual images in your project as you build it, making changes along the way as needed. To change settings, double-click the Levels thumbnail icon in the Layers palette to redisplay the Levels dialog (see Figure 4.25).

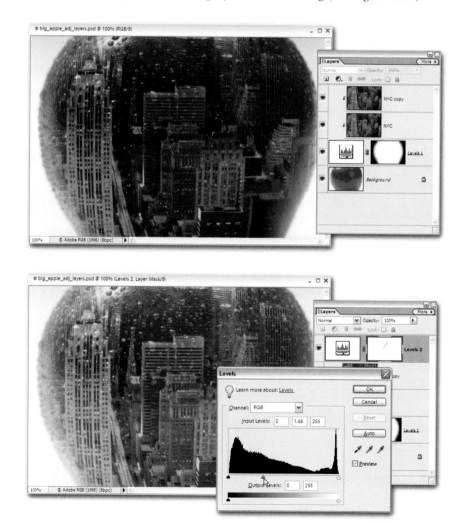

Figure 4.25 Adding the New York City photos made the image much too dark. By adding a Levels adjustment layer (top) and moving the midtone slider in the new layer's Levels dialog to the left (bottom), we make the image much lighter.

Brightness/Contrast This type of adjustment layer allows you to make nondestructive tonal adjustments using the Brightness/Contrast dialog (see Figure 4.26). You should use this adjustment layer only to adjust small portions of an image rather than all of it. The Brightness/Contrast controls are too limited to make overall image tonal adjustments. In general, the best way to make tonal adjustments is to use the Levels adjustment layer.

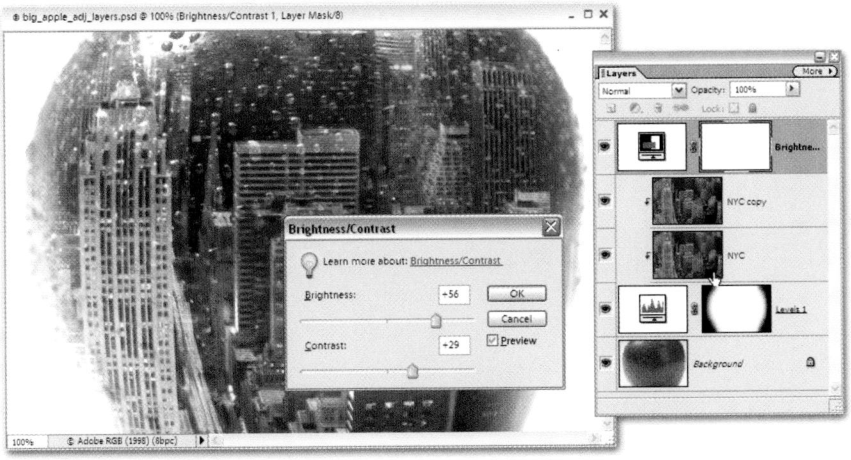

Figure 4.26 The Brightness/Contrast dialog does not offer as much tonal control as the Levels dialog.

Hue/Saturation This type of adjustment layer allows you to make nondestructive color adjustments using the Hue/Saturation dialog. By moving the sliders, you can adjust the hue (color), saturation (purity), and lightness information of an entire image, or one of its colors (Red, Green, Blue, Cyan, Magenta, or Yellow). To apply a Hue/Saturation adjustment to the entire image, keep Master selected in the Edit menu; otherwise, choose a color from the menu list. The two color bars at the bottom of the dialog correspond to the sequence of colors on the color wheel. The top bar displays the color before any adjustments are made. The bottom color bar displays any hue, saturation, and lightness adjustments that are made.

As they do with tonality, the colors of your image can change dramatically as you add layers to a project. With Hue/Saturation adjustment layers, you can color-correct individual images in your project as you build it, and make changes along the way as needed. To modify these settings, double-click the Hue/Saturation thumbnail icon in the Layers palette to redisplay the Hue/Saturation dialog (see Figure 4.27).

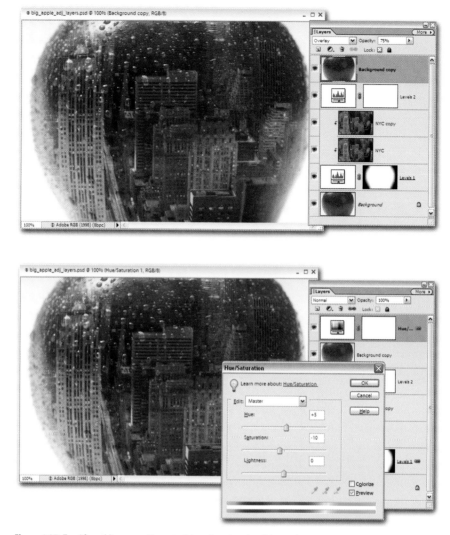

Figure 4.27 Top: After adding several layers to this project, the color of the apple appears more magenta than red. Bottom: Adding a Hue/Saturation adjustment layer and moving the Hue slider to the right (+5) and the Saturation slider to the left (-10) corrects the color.

Gradient Map   This type of adjustment layer allows you to map an image's corresponding grayscale range to a vibrant gradient fill. When you add a Gradient Map layer, Elements automatically displays the Gradient Map dialog. This dialog allows you to choose a gradient to map the image to. To access the dialog and change the gradient at any time, double-click the Gradient Map thumbnail icon in the Layers palette. You can use Gradient Map layers to create special color effects like the one shown in Figure 4.28.

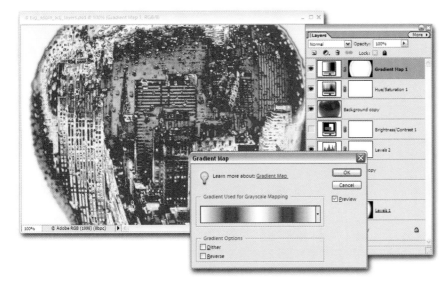

Figure 4.28 Adding a custom red-and-white Gradient Map layer created this effect.

Photo Filter   This type of adjustment layer allows you to emulate the same filters professional photographers use to correct tainted color temperature. When adding a Photo Filter layer, Elements automatically displays the Photo Filter dialog. In this dialog you can choose a warming or cooling filter to apply to your image. You can also control the density of the filter by moving the slider at the bottom of the dialog. The Preserve Luminosity option applies the color effect without altering density. Disabling this option darkens the effect. To access the dialog and change the filter or density setting at any time, double-click the Photo Filter thumbnail icon in the Layers palette.

You can use warming filters to remove blue color casts, or add emphasis to warm images such as a sunrise or sunset. Cooling filters can remove yellow or orange color casts, or accentuate the cold nature of images such as a winter scene (see Figure 4.29).

Figure 4.29 Top: This photograph of a winter scene is nice, but the chilliness of the snow could be accentuated. Bottom: A Photo Filter layer with the Cooling filter (82) applied adds a slight blue cast to the snow, thereby emphasizing the cool nature of the subject.

Invert   This type of adjustment layer allows you to reverse an image to take on the appearance of a film negative (see Figure 4.30). There are no settings for this adjustment layer; therefore, when adding it to a document, no dialog is displayed.

Threshold   This type of adjustment layer allows you to create a high-contrast, black-and-white representation of an image. When you add a Threshold adjustment layer, Elements automatically displays the Threshold dialog. By moving the slider under the histogram all the way to the left, you can locate the darkest areas of the photo. By moving it all the way to the right, you can locate the lightest areas (see Figure 4.31).

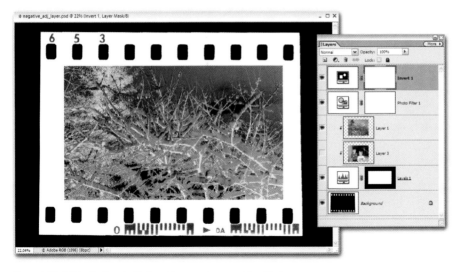

Figure 4.30 Adding the Invert adjustment layer creates a negative effect.

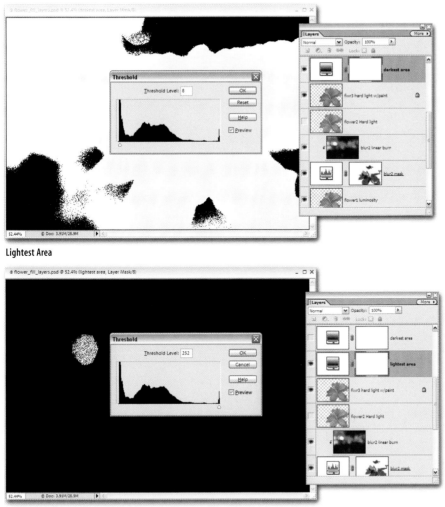

Lightest Area

Darkest Area

Figure 4.31 You can use the Threshold adjustment layer to locate the darkest and lightest areas of a photo.

Locating the darkest/lightest areas of a photo using this method can assist you in creating a Levels adjustment layer. Now that you've located these areas, you can turn off visibility for the Threshold layers and set the black point/white point with the Eyedroppers in the Levels dialog. Doing so helps bring out the detail in over saturated areas. You can gain even more control over which areas are affected by the Levels adjustment by painting in the layer mask with a soft brush (see Figure 4.32).

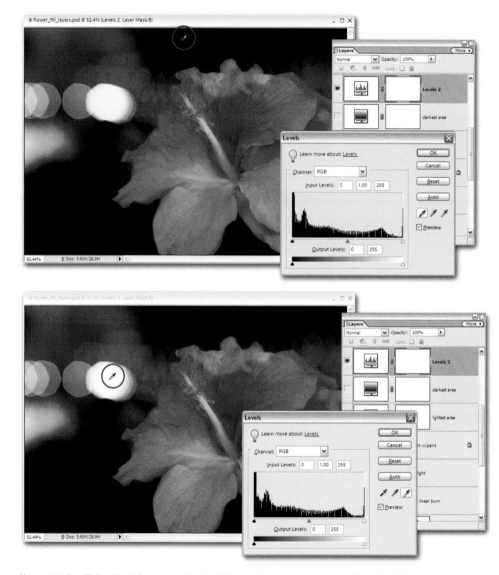

Figure 4.32 Top: Click in the darkest areas with the Set Black Point eyedropper. Bottom: Click in the lightest areas with the Set White Point eyedropper.

Continued on next page

Figure 4.32 *(Continued)* Paint inside the Levels adjustment layer mask with a soft brush to control which areas are affected.

Posterize   This type of adjustment layer allows you to control the number of tonal levels applied to each color channel. When you add a Posterize adjustment layer, Elements automatically displays the Posterize dialog. Enter a number in the Levels field and check the preview option to see the effect as it is applied. Lower numbers can radically change the look and feel of an image (see Figure 4.33). To access the dialog and change the level setting at any time, double-click the Posterize thumbnail icon in the Layers palette.

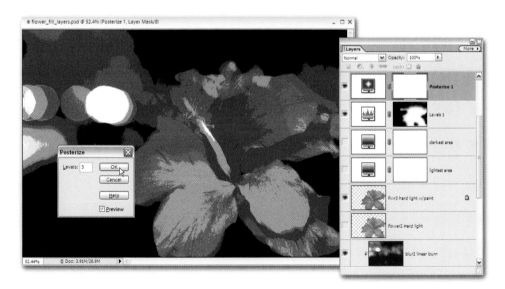

Figure 4.33 Applying lower values in the Posterize dialog can create some exciting effects.

Managing Layers

One thing to remember as you add image layers to your composition is that by doing so, you are also adding to the overall file size of the document. The more images you add, the larger the file gets. The larger the file gets, the harder Photoshop Elements has to work to manage the file. It doesn't take long for a layered file to grow and quickly eat up space on your hard drive, especially if it's set up at a higher resolution and larger print size.

Here are a few precautions you can take to keep Elements running smoothly and prevent your hard drive from filling up:

- Back up your layered files regularly to CD, DVD, or to an external drive.

- Always try to leave at least 1 GB of hard drive space available at all times, and never let it fill up entirely.

- Be sure to monitor the file size of your projects as you work on them. You can do so by clicking the right-facing black arrow at the bottom of the document window and choosing Document Sizes from the fly-out menu. The number on the right indicates the current size of the layered file. The number on the left indicates what the size of the file will be if the image is flattened.

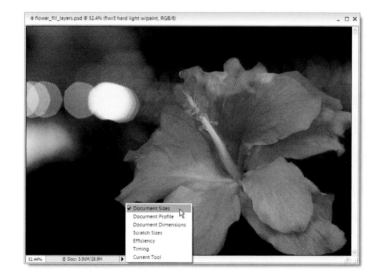

- If your layered composition becomes enormous, consider merging layers if possible. Be sure to only merge those layers that you are certain will not need further adjustments made to them.

Merging and Flattening Layers

Images that do not need to remain on their own layers can be merged into a single layer in order to keep file size down and conserve drive space. Several merge commands are available in Photoshop Elements:

Merge Down To merge a single selected layer with the layer beneath it in the Layers palette, choose Merge Down from the Layer menu, the palette Merge Down from the

Layer menu, the palette menu, or the selected layer's right-click context menu. Note that if either layer is part of a separate group, or if both layers contain any combination of effect, shape, or type layers, the Merge Down command cannot be applied (use Merge Layers instead). Effect, shape, and type layers can only be merged down if the layer below is an image layer that is not part of a separate group. You *can* apply the Merge Down command to compatible layers that *are* part of the same group.

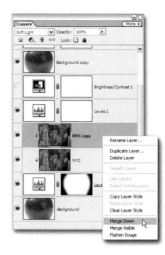

Note: The keyboard shortcut for Merge Down and Merge Layers is Ctrl+E (Windows) or ⌘+E (Mac).

Merge Layers   To merge multiple selected layers, contiguous or noncontiguous, choose Merge Layers from the Layer menu, the palette menu, or the layer's right-click context menu. You can merge selected layers of any type as long as one or more of them is not part of a separate group. As you can with Merge Down, you can apply the Merge Down command to compatible layers that are part of the same group. Once the command is applied, the selected layers below are merged into the topmost selected layer in the stack.

Merge Visible   To merge all visible layers, choose Merge Visible from the Layer menu, the palette menu, or the right-click context menu. By applying this command, Elements merges all visible layers into the bottommost visible layer in the stack—underneath all of the remaining hidden layers.

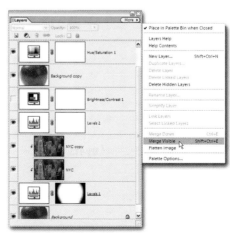

Note: The keyboard shortcut for Merge Visible is Shift+Ctrl+E (Windows) or Shift+⌘+E (Mac).

Using Merged Layers as Layer Comps

It is also possible to merge selected layers while maintaining layer separations in a document. Although this actually adds to the file size rather than conserving it, you can use these merged layers to test whether your transparency effects will look the same when flattened. You can also use these merged layers to create different merged versions of your design ideas, similar to working with the Layer Comps palette in Elements' big brother application, Photoshop CS2. To do so, select the layers, hold down the Alt key (Windows) or Option key (Mac), and choose Merge Layers from the Layer menu, palette menu, or context menu. The new merged layer is positioned above the topmost selected layer.

Flatten Image   To merge all layers into a single flattened layer, choose Flatten image from the Layer menu, the palette menu, or the right-click context menu. Before you do, though, be aware that this is a risky move. You really only want to flatten an image's layers when you are finished building your composition, and even then, you should issue the Save As command first and then flatten the image. Doing so ensures that you always have a working copy of your layered file.

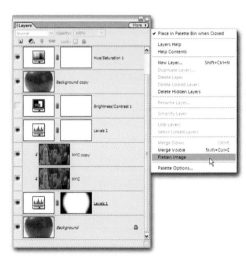

Deleting Unused Layers

Another way to keep the file size of your projects down is to delete unused layers. Elements offers a variety of ways to do this.

   To delete a single selected layer, or multiple selected layers, choose Delete Layer from the Layer menu, the palette menu, or the context menu. You can also click the trashcan icon at the top of the Layers palette, or drag the selected layers directly over it (see Figure 4.34).

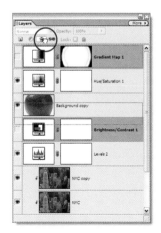

Figure 4.34
Drag the selected layers over the trashcan icon to delete them.

Two other delete commands are only accessible through the Layers palette menu:

Delete Linked Layers This command allows you to trash one or more linked groups at a time. To delete all layers in a linked group, select at least one of the layers in the group and choose Delete Linked Layers from the palette menu. To delete more than one linked group, you must have at least one linked layer from each group selected (see Figure 4.35).

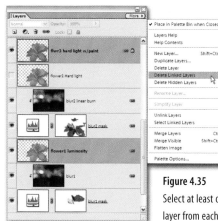

Figure 4.35
Select at least one layer from each linked group and choose Delete Linked Layers from the palette menu.

Delete Hidden Layers This command allows you to trash all hidden layers in a document. You do not have to select any hidden layers in the palette in order to delete them with this command. After choosing Delete Hidden Layers, a warning dialog appears asking if you are sure you want to delete them. Click Yes only if you are certain that that the hidden layers do not contain images or adjustments that you might want to use later; otherwise, click No to keep them. If you don't want this dialog to appear every time you apply the command, click the Don't Show Again option before clicking Yes or No (see Figure 4.36).

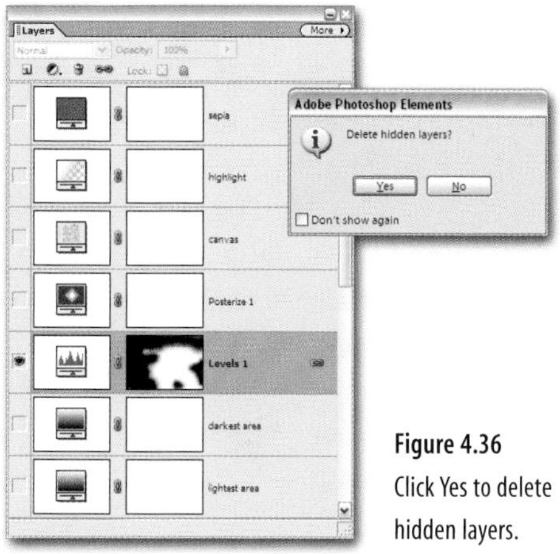

Figure 4.36
Click Yes to delete hidden layers.

The Power of
Opacity and Blending

In some of the example projects described in the previous chapters, we showed how you can enhance the creativity of your layered compositions using layer opacity and blend modes. In this chapter, we'll take a much closer look at the Layers palette and explore how you can use it to adjust the opacity value for individual layers in a composition. This palette offers you incredible flexibility when combining images. You can also use the Layers palette to change the way layers interact with each other by applying different blend modes. You can even create special effects by experimenting with various blend mode combinations.

5

Chapter Contents
Adjusting Layer Opacity
Applying Blend Modes

Adjusting Layer Opacity

Every layer that you add to a composition shares a specific relationship with the other layers surrounding it in the Layers palette. One very straightforward way that you can blend layers together and control the way they interact is by adjusting each layer's opacity level.

To understand layer opacity, it helps if you think of layers as the building blocks of your project. Painting with oil paint on a canvas is a good analogy. To paint your masterpiece, you must add paint to the canvas and blend colors together along the way. Doing so helps to unify the overall image. The same principles apply when you're creating a layered composition in Photoshop Elements. Consider the layers that you're adding as your oil paint and the document window as your canvas. You can use the Opacity control in the Layers palette to blend layers together and unify your image.

Located at the top of the Layers palette, the Opacity control allows you to make a selected layer completely or partly transparent. By default, all new layers added to a composition are set to 100% Opacity. Lowering the opacity value allows you to see through to the layers underneath in the stack (see Figure 5.1).

You can lower the opacity value of a selected layer in the palette either by entering a number in the Opacity field or by clicking the arrow to the right of the field and dragging the pop-up slider control to the left (see Figure 5.2).

Scrubbing

You can also raise or lower dynamic field values in the Elements interface using a technique called "scrubbing." To change a setting using this method, start out by hovering the mouse cursor over the field label, such as Opacity in the Layers palette. When the cursor changes to display a hand with left/right arrows on either side of it, click and drag to the left (to decrease) or right (to increase). To adjust values in 10% increments, hold down the Shift key as you click and drag.

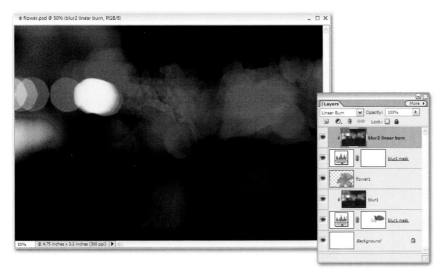

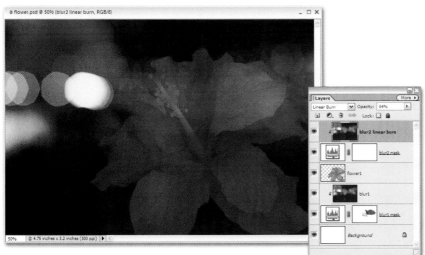

Figure 5.1 Top: The blurred city image at the top of the layer stack has the Linear Burn blend mode applied to it. This makes the layer partially transparent, but not transparent enough to see clearly through to the flower image layer underneath. Bottom: Reducing the opacity of the blurred city layer to 64% makes the flower image underneath much more apparent.

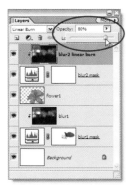

Figure 5.2
To reduce a selected layer's opacity using the pop-up slider, click the arrow next to the opacity value and drag the bar to the left. The opacity change is displayed in the document window as you scroll.

You can adjust the opacity value of a selected layer in 10% increments using the number keys or the numeric keypad. To change the value using this method, access any tool that does not have its own opacity settings, such as the Move tool, and then press 1 to apply a value of 10%, 2 for 20%, 3 for 30%, and so forth. Press 0 to apply a value of 100%. You can also type two numbers quickly in succession in order to apply a specific value (e.g., typing 85 applies a value of 85%).

Note: You can only adjust the opacity value of a single selected layer at a time. You cannot adjust the opacity value for multiple selected layers.

Examples: Creating Shadows and Softening Focus

Controlling layer opacity is a fundamental technique for combining images, and we'll continue to use it in examples throughout the remaining chapters. Before we move on to survey the different blend modes, however, it will be instructive to focus on a couple of specific effects you can achieve with layer opacity: adding shadows and softening focus.

Creating Photorealistic Shadows

The sequence of screens in Figure 5.3 shows how you can convert filled selections into photorealistic shadows and highlights by adjusting layer opacity. In the example, a new layer is created; then a selection is loaded and filled with black. To make the filled area appear as a shadow, the opacity level of the layer is reduced to 42%.

1

Figure 5.3 1. Combining the image of the girl with the torn paper image creates a neat effect, but to make the image appear more realistic, we must add a shadow layer. 2. To create the effect of shadows cast by the paper onto the girl's portrait, we first make a selection of the areas where shadows would fall, save the selection as a new layer, and fill it with black. 3. Once we deselect and reduce the layer's opacity level to 42%, the filled area begins to take on the appearance of a shadow. 4. To complete the effect, we change the blend mode to Multiply and apply a slight Motion Blur filter (for more on filters, see Chapter 8).

Continued on next page

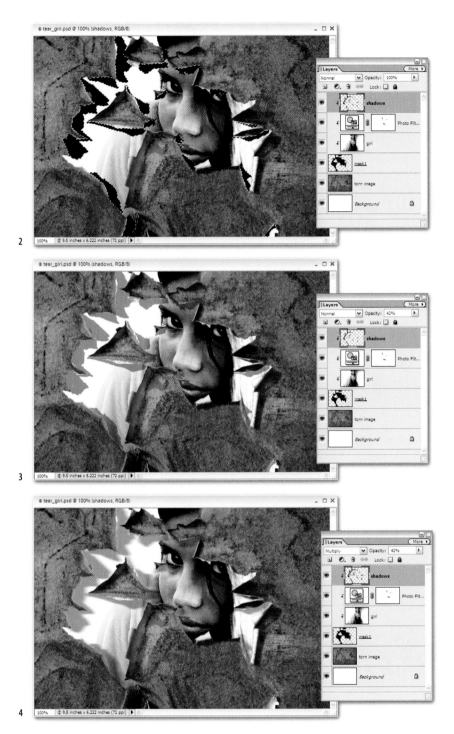

Figure 5.3 *(Continued)*

In the previous chapter you saw that one of the fundamental advantages of working with layers is that your edits are *nondestructive*—they don't change any of the original pixel information. In particular, you can use layer opacity to adjust the focus of an
image nondestructively. In the example shown in Figure 5.4, I duplicated a transparent

image layer, positioned it above the original in the stack, and then applied a Gaussian Blur filter to the duplicate layer. Lowering the blurred layer's opacity level begins to reveal the original detailed image below. The combination of the two creates a soft-focus effect.

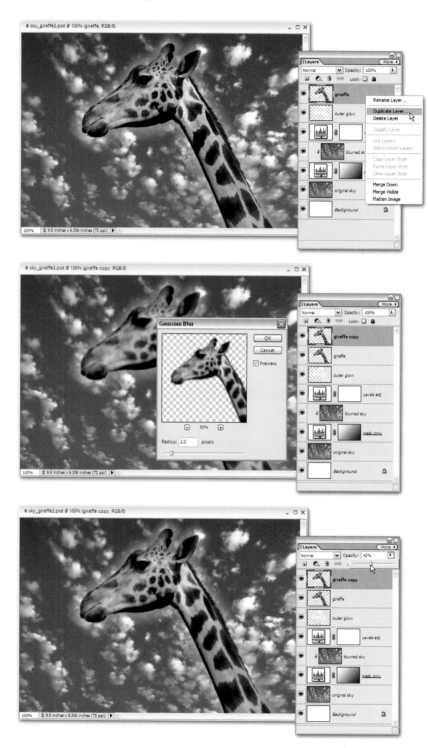

Figure 5.4 Top: The giraffe layer is duplicated. Middle: A 2-pixel Gaussian Blur filter is applied to the duplicate layer. Bottom: Lowering the duplicate layer's opacity level to 42% creates a nondestructive soft focus effect.

Applying Blend Modes

Blend modes give you further control over the way layers interact with each other in a composition. Try combining applied blend modes with layer opacity adjustments and masking, and you'll soon realize how much creative control you really have. By experimenting with various blend mode combinations, you can fine-tune specific areas of an image and even create special effects.

To apply a blend mode, first select a layer; then click the blend mode field (or the down-facing arrow next to it) at the top of the Layers palette to reveal a pop-up menu. Highlight the desired blend mode from the menu and click to apply it.

A Quick Tour of the Blend Modes

Photoshop Elements offers more than 20 different blend modes, so before you begin experimenting, it's a good idea to familiarize yourself with the various modes and how they work. Here's a brief description of what each blend mode does, using our "flower and street lights" image as the example (in these shots, the flower is the selected image layer, and the street lights are in the background layer below it).

Essentially, the blend modes control how—or whether—the color in the selected layer interacts with that of the layers below it. They all work by looking at pixel information for a given location in the two layers, but they differ in both the type of information they work with and the general effect they have on an image. Some compare luminosity (grayscale) values, where 0 is black, 128 is 50% gray, and 255 is white. Others compare RGB or HSV values. Likewise, some tend to darken or lighten the resulting image, while others tend to enhance or reduce contrast, or to make other changes. The main point to keep in mind about blend modes is that Multiply drops the whites, Screen drops the blacks, and Overlay blends everything. Once you know this, you can determine which blend mode you want to apply, since most of the blend modes (except for Dissolve and the bottom photographic set—Hue, Saturation, Luminosity, etc.) are based on these three.

Except where noted otherwise, the descriptions that follow assume that the selected layer is at 100% opacity.

Previewing Blend Modes

To preview each blend mode effect as it is applied to your project, select a layer in the Layers palette, and then click in the blend mode field to highlight the current mode selection. Press the up/down arrow keys to scroll through the list and preview each effect. Press Enter to apply the desired blend mode to the layer.

Normal At 100% opacity, the selected layer's color does not blend with that of the layers beneath it.

Dissolve At less than 100% opacity, Dissolve displays some pixels of the selected layer at 100% opacity, but displays random pixels as completely transparent. As you lower the opacity value of the selected layer, more pixels are replaced by the lower layer's color.

Darken   Wherever the selected layer's color is lighter than that of the pixels in the layer underneath, the darker color is applied.

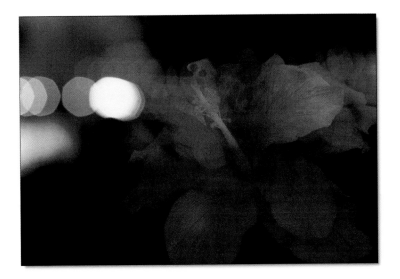

Multiply   Darkens the resulting image in proportion to the grayscale value of the selected layer; 25% gray makes the underlying layer 25% darker, 50% gray makes it 50% darker, and so on. Dark colors are forced to black, and white is not affected.

Color Burn   Applies the hue of the pixels in the lower layer to those of the selected layer. Color Burn has a greater effect on darker colors.

Linear Burn   By applying the brightness of the selected layer, Linear Burn darkens the color of the underlying layer. White has no effect. The result is similar to Multiply but more intense.

Lighten Wherever the selected layer's color is darker than the colors contained in the layers underneath, the lighter color is applied.

Screen The inverse of Multiply, this adds brightness. It lightens the resulting color in proportion to the luminosity of the selected layer. Screening lighter colors produces greater changes; black is not affected.

Color Dodge   Colorizes a selected layer's pixels using the hue of the pixels in the layers underneath. Color Dodge has a greater effect on lighter colors than darker ones.

Linear Dodge   The opposite of Linear Burn, Linear Dodge lightens the colors contained in the layers underneath by applying the brightness of the selected layer. Black has no effect.

Note: A blend mode selection can only be applied to a single selected layer at a time, not to multiple selected layers.

Overlay Darkens (multiplies) or lightens (screens) a selected layer's color while preserving highlights and shadows. Contrasting colors produce greater changes; black, white, and 50% gray are not affected.

Soft Light Darkens (multiplies) or lightens (screens) a selected layer's color without preserving highlight and shadow values. All colors in the selected layer that are darker than 50% gray darken the colors contained in the layers underneath; colors lighter than 50% gray lighten them. Black, white, and 50% gray are not affected.

Hard Light   Produces the same effect as Soft Light (see the earlier description), except with more contrast.

Vivid Light   Reduces contrast in the lighter areas of the selected layer (below 50% gray) and increases contrast in the darker areas (above 50% gray).

Note: Blend modes can also be applied to fill and adjustment layers.

Linear Light   Decreases brightness in the lighter areas of the selected layer (below 50% gray) and increases brightness in the darker areas (above 50% gray).

Pin Light   The colors of the layers underneath are replaced by the selected layer's colors, based on the lightness and darkness values for both.

Hard Mix   Applies a posterize effect based on the selected layer's opacity value. Higher values produce stronger results.

Difference   Applies the color that results when the selected layer's color and the colors underneath are subtracted from each other. White inverts the colors contained in the layers underneath; black has no effect.

Exclusion   Produces the same effect as Difference, but with less contrast.

Hue   Applies the hue of the selected layer's color to the luminance and saturation of the colors contained in the layers underneath.

Saturation   Applies the saturation of the selected layer's color to the luminance and hue of the colors contained in the layers underneath.

Color   Applies the hue and saturation of the selected layer's color to the luminance of the colors contained in the layers underneath.

Luminosity Applies the luminance of the selected layer's color to the hue and saturation of the colors contained in the layers underneath.

Example: Interactive Blend Modes

Now that you're familiar with all of the various blend modes and what they can do, here's an example of how we can use some of them to blend layers together in a composition. The following example combines two images using blend modes, layer opacity, and adjustment layers. I'll describe the process used to create the "Big Apple" composite first seen in Chapter 3. If you follow along with two of your own images, you'll probably need to adjust some of the settings.

1. I first selected the image area to be used for a mask, using the Selection Brush in Mask mode (see Chapter 2, "Making Good Selections") and then softened the selection edge by applying a feather amount of 10 pixels (see Chapter 3, "Modifying Selections").

2. To reset the default colors of black foreground and white background, I clicked the Default Foreground and Background button at the bottom of the Tools palette. I then inverted the selection (Ctrl+Shift+I—Win / ⌘+Shift+I—Mac) and created a new layer (by clicking the Create A New Layer button at the top of the Layers palette) and filled the feathered selection with white (Ctrl+Backspace—Win / ⌘+Delete—Mac). I named the layer "white feathered mask" so that it can be easily identified.

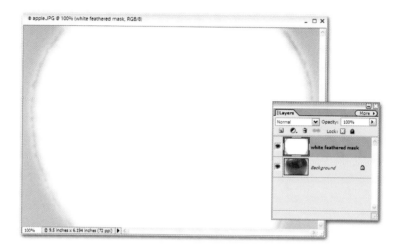

3. I deselected the layer (Ctrl+D—Win / ⌘+D—Mac) and changed its layer blend mode to Soft Light in order to lighten the colors in the apple image underneath.

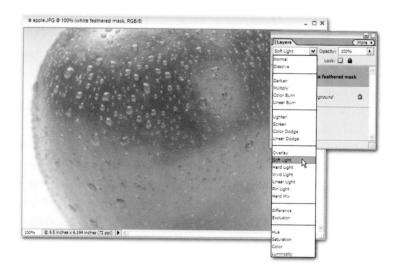

4. I imported the New York City image into the document using the drag-and-drop technique (see Chapter 4, "Mastering Layers," for more on drag-and-drop), and positioned it above the "white feathered mask" layer. Pressing Ctrl+Shift+U (Win) / ⌘+Shift+U (Mac) desaturated the image. To add some roundness, I applied the Spherize filter (Filter > Distort > Spherize). For more on filters, see Chapter 8, "Adding Filters, Styles, and Effects."

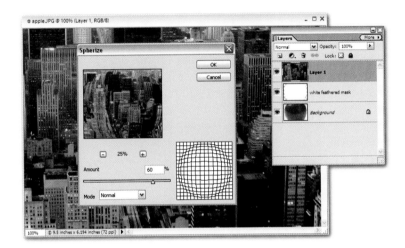

5. I changed the layer blend mode to Multiply and renamed the layer "NYC 100% Multiply." Changing the blend mode to Multiply allows you to see through the NYC image to the apple underneath. All of the white areas drop out of the image.

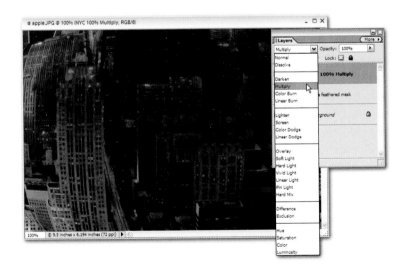

6. I grouped the desaturated NYC image to the "white feathered mask" layer using the Group command (Ctrl+G—Win / ⌘+G—Mac); I could also have Alt / Opt-clicked between layers in the Layers palette.

7. In this example, the NYC image is not dark enough and does not stand out over the apple. To correct this, I duplicated the image by pressing Ctrl+J (Win) / ⌘+J (Mac), and changed the duplicate layer's blend mode to Overlay. Doing so darkens the NYC image. I renamed the layer "NYC 100% Overlay."

8. I again used Ctrl+G (Win) / ⌘+G (Mac) to add the duplicate NYC image to the group.

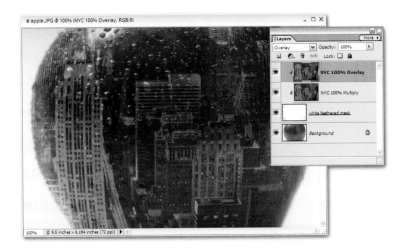

9. I then added a Levels adjustment layer. To do this, you first Alt / Opt-click the Adjustment Layer icon, and then select Layers from the pop-up menu. In the resulting New Layer dialog, select the Group With Previous Layer option. Click OK to create the adjustment layer and add it to the clipping group, which prohibits the Levels adjustment made in the next step from affecting any regions outside of the masked area.

10. In the Levels dialog that appears, I set the input levels to 5 (for the black point), 2.11 (for the neutral gray point), and 218 (for the white point). These values lighten the mid-tones and heighten the contrast for the overall image, including all of the layers underneath. Clicking OK closes the dialog and applies the layer adjustment.

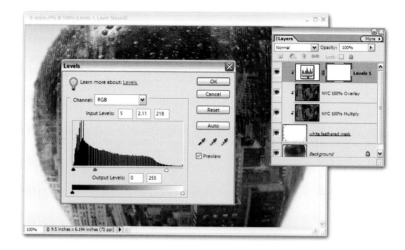

11. In the Layers palette, I selected the Background image, duplicated it (Ctrl+J— Win / ⌘+J—Mac), and moved the duplicate layer to the top of the layer stack.

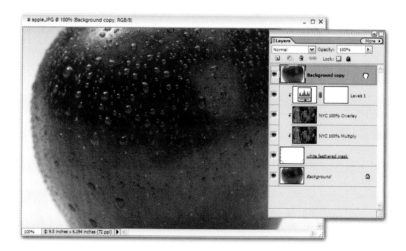

12. To bring some of the red color back to the apple, I changed the duplicate layer's blend mode to Overlay. Doing so makes the layer transparent, but also oversaturates the image's overall color. To correct this, I reduced the layer opacity level to 75% (and renamed the layer "apple overlay 75%.")

13. The background surrounding the apple is now completely white. To restore the background to its original state, a layer mask must be applied to the apple overlay layer. To do this, I used the trick (introduced in Chapter 2) of creating a new adjustment layer just for its layer mask. I selected the Levels adjustment layer below the apple overlay layer by clicking it in the Layers palette, and then created a new Levels adjustment layer by clicking the Adjustment Layer icon and selecting Levels from the pop-up menu. I made no adjustments and simply closed the dialog by clicking OK. I created a new group by Alt/Opt-clicking between the new Levels adjustment layer and the apple overlay layer above it in the Layers palette.

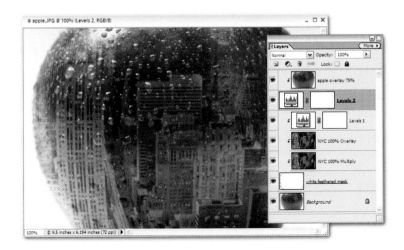

14. I then masked out the background area surrounding the apple by Ctrl / ⌘-clicking the "white feathered mask" layer to select everything on the layer; inverting the selection (Ctrl+Shift+I—Win / ⌘+Shift+I—Mac); and filling the selection with black in the new Levels adjustment layer mask by pressing Alt+Backspace—Win / Opt+Backspace—Mac. The original background area color is now restored. I can deselect the area by pressing Ctrl+D—Win / ⌘+D—Mac.

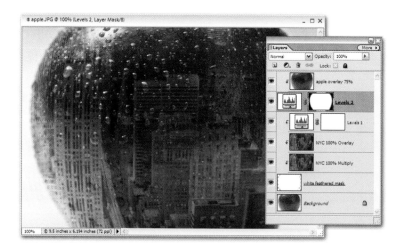

15. To enhance the color of the overall image, I added a Hue and Saturation adjustment level at the top of the layer stack. In the Hue / Saturation dialog, I raised the Hue setting to +5, which gives the apple's red color a warmer tone. I also decreased the Saturation setting to -10, which takes away some of the brightness of the color. Clicking OK closes the dialog and applies the layer adjustment.

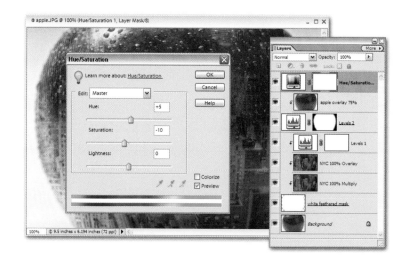

16. The layered composition is complete! I successfully combined the images by using blend modes, adjustment layers, and adjustment layer masks.

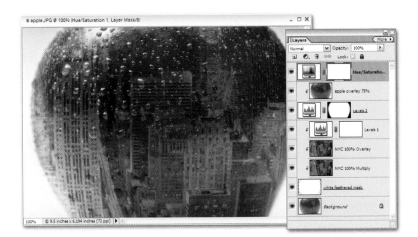

Note: The accompanying CD-ROM includes a video lesson on applying blend modes and adjusting layer opacity.

Compositing with Masks

Along with layer opacity controls and layer blend modes, layer masks are another important tool for combining images in Photoshop Elements. Masks allow you to conceal (or reveal) specific image areas in a layered composition, and they work nondestructively. They really are the ultimate creative safety net, giving you the ability to try out all of your ideas before permanently altering any pixels. In this chapter, we'll look at how you can use layer masks along with brushes, gradients, filters, and filled selections. We'll also see how you can use clipping masks to place images inside text characters or other shapes.

Chapter Contents

What Is a Mask?

In the days before digital photography, a physical mask (such as a sheet of paper) was placed over unexposed photographic film in a darkroom to prevent stray or unwanted light from reaching specific areas of an image. This technique allowed the photographer to darken or completely hide a portion of the image. In Photoshop Elements, you can achieve the same effect by adding variations of gray to a *layer mask*. You can also use layer masks to control which areas of an image are affected by layer adjustment effects (such as Levels, Hue/Saturation, etc.). As you've seen throughout the earlier chapters, Elements automatically creates a layer mask along with every fill and adjustment layer that you add to a composition (Figure 6.1).

Layer Mask

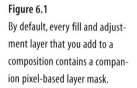

Figure 6.1

By default, every fill and adjustment layer that you add to a composition contains a companion pixel-based layer mask.

Black Conceals, White Reveals

When you're working with adjustment layer masks, it's important to understand that *black conceals* and *white reveals*. Any area of a layer mask containing 100% black *conceals* those portions of the image, so that the layers below it in the Layers palette *are not* affected by the adjustment. Any area containing 100% white *reveals* those portions of the image, so that the layers below *are* affected by the adjustment. Shades of gray in a layer mask *partially* conceal those areas of the image, so that the layers below are affected in proportion to the grayscale value (see Figure 6.2).

What this means is that you can control which areas of your image are affected by an adjustment layer by painting in the companion layer mask with the Brush tool, or by filling selections in the mask with a color or gradient (see Figure 6.3).

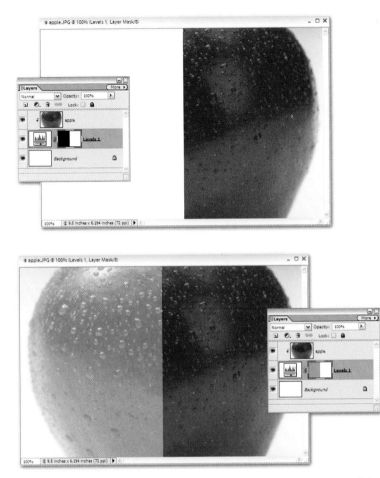

Figure 6.2 Top: Black conceals a masked area; white reveals it. Bottom: Shades of gray partially hide the adjustment.

Painted
— Layer
Mask

Figure 6.3 Painting in each of the grouped adjustment layer masks with the Brush tool helped create this image by allowing me to control which areas of the two blur layers were interacting with the two flower layers.

Clipping Masks and Groups

You can also group image layers that are positioned directly above an adjustment layer in the Layers palette, creating what is known as a *clipping mask*. Adding several images to a clipping mask makes it a *clipping group* (see Figure 6.4). Once the clipping mask or group is created, you can control how image layers blend together by painting in the layer mask with the Brush tool, or by filling selections in the mask with a color or gradient.

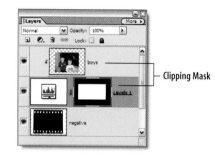

— Clipping Mask

— Clipping Group

Figure 6.4

In a clipping mask (top), the black and gray areas mask out the contents of the grouped layer above. The adjustment layer containing the mask (a.k.a. the base layer) always appears with its name underlined. The thumbnail of the grouped layer above always appears indented. In a clipping group (bottom), the black and gray areas mask out the contents of multiple contiguous layers positioned directly above in the layer stack.

It's important to understand that in Photoshop Elements, you can only gain access to a layer mask by adding an adjustment layer. The reason all adjustment layers contain a layer mask by default is so that you can use it to control which areas of the image are affected by the adjustment. But in addition, you can use some of these adjustment layer masks to hide or reveal portions of an image by grouping them to the image layers above them in the Layers palette.

You cannot apply a layer mask directly to a layer as you can in Elements' big brother application, Photoshop CS2. In Elements, the only way to apply a mask directly to an image layer is to use the following procedure:

1. Add a Levels, Hue and Saturation, or Brightness/Contrast adjustment layer. These are the only three adjustment layers that will not affect your image if no adjustment is made in the dialog. All other adjustment layers can change your image even if no adjustment is made.

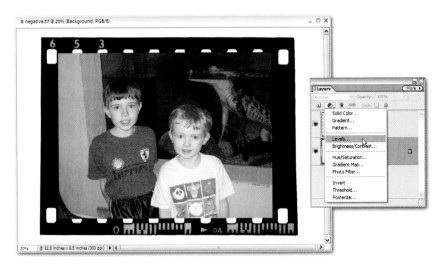

2. Click OK to bypass the adjustment layer dialog. Do not make any adjustments before clicking OK.

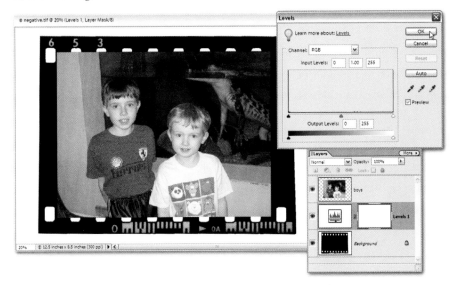

3. Position the new adjustment layer directly underneath the image layer in the palette.

4. Group the image layer to the adjustment layer using the Group command (Ctrl+G—Win / ⌘+G—Mac), or by Alt/Option-clicking between layers in the Layers palette.

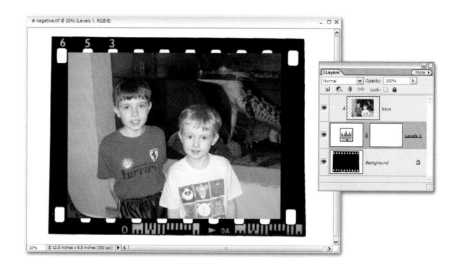

5. Proceed to paint in the layer mask with the Brush tool, or fill a selection in the mask with a color or gradient. Be sure to click directly on the layer mask thumbnail in the Layers palette to ensure that you are working in the mask. Elements places an outline around the layer mask thumbnail when the mask is activated.

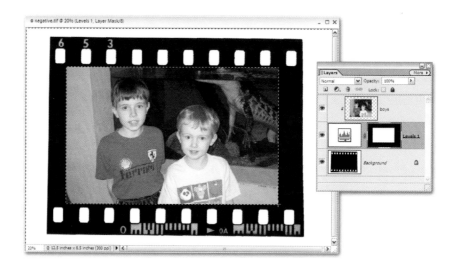

It is also possible to group image layers together without including an adjustment layer mask. The following is a step-by-step example of how two images can be combined using a traditional image layer clipping group.

1.   Create a new layer in between the two image layers that you would like to mask. Be sure to give the layer a descriptive name, such as "Mask 1."

2.   Make a selection of the area you would like to mask using any of the selection tools (see Chapter 2, "Making Good Selections"). In this example, I've used the Rectangular Marquee tool.

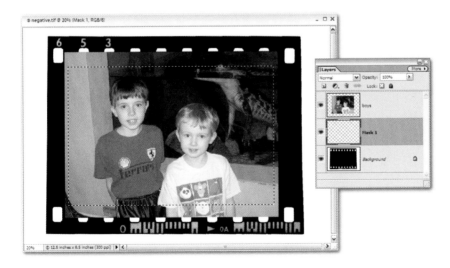

3. Fill the selection with a color. Notice that when layers are grouped this way, the image above is cropped inside the filled area of the base layer below. All pixels in the surrounding transparent area of the base layer are concealed.

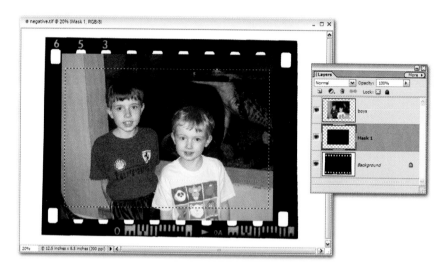

4. Group the image layer to the adjustment layer using the Group command (Ctrl+G—Win / ⌘+G—Mac), or by Alt/Option-clicking between layers in the Layers palette. If necessary, reposition the grouped image inside the cropped area with the Move tool.

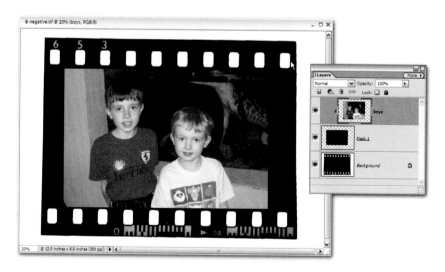

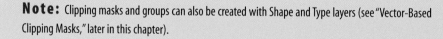

Note: Clipping masks and groups can also be created with Shape and Type layers (see "Vector-Based Clipping Masks," later in this chapter).

Blending with Masks and Groups

Once you group an image layer to an adjustment layer containing a mask (using the previously described method), there are several blending techniques you can use to combine images in a layered composition.

You can hide specific areas of a composite image by painting in layer masks with the Brush tool, or filling selections in the mask with a color or gradient. You can also feather or blur a selection in a grouped layer mask. Unlike adjusting layer opacity or applying layer blend modes, these are much more hands-on techniques for controlling how image layers interact with each other.

Filling Selections in a Layer Mask

One of the easiest ways to combine image layers is to fill a selection in a grouped layer mask. Here's where knowing how to make good selections really comes in handy. You can use any of the selection tools in the Tools palette to make your initial selection. Just be sure you have the layer mask selected in the layers palette *before* you fill the selection; otherwise, you will wind up filling the selection on the image layer and not the mask. You can tell when the layer mask is selected by the outline that appears around its thumbnail in the palette.

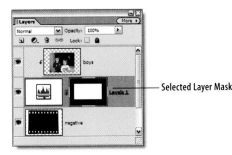

— Selected Layer Mask

As an example, the following steps show how I used a filled, elliptical marquee selection to mask one photograph inside another, creating the "cueball with bound hands" composite first seen in Chapter 2, "Making Good Selections."

1. With the cueball image open, I made an Elliptical Marquee tool selection (see Chapter 2) to define the area to be masked.

2. I added a Levels adjustment layer simply to gain access to its companion layer mask. I made no adjustments and bypassed the adjustment layer dialog by clicking OK.

3. The layer mask is automatically filled with black in the areas surrounding the elliptical selection, as shown by the layer mask thumbnail in the Layers palette.

4. I imported the tied-hands image shape into the document using the drag-and-drop technique (see Chapter 4, "Mastering Layers"), and positioned it above the Levels adjustment layer in the Layers palette. I renamed the layer "tied-hands 1."

5. I grouped the selected tied-hands image layer to the Levels adjustment layer below it by using the Group command (Ctrl+G—Win / ⌘+G—Mac); I could also have grouped them by Alt/Option-clicking between layers in the Layers palette. I then used the Move tool to reposition the tied hands image in the layer mask.

6. To add some roundness to the tied-hands image, I applied the Spherize filter by choosing Filter > Distort > Spherize (for more on filters, see Chapter 8, "Adding Filters, Styles, and Effects").

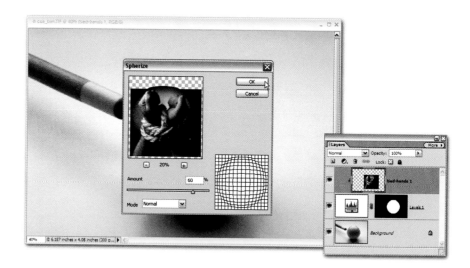

7. To make the tied-hands image layer blend in better with the cueball image underneath, I changed its blend mode to Soft Light. I then duplicated the image to make it stand out better, and changed the duplicate's blend mode to Hard Light. I added the duplicate to the group by Alt/Option-clicking between the layers in the Layers palette.

 Note: Sometimes changing the layer blend mode can create a cool effect, but it may not be strong enough. When this happens, try duplicating the layer, and then adjust the duplicate layer's opacity level as needed. This can be used as a "hands-on" technique for intensifying a blend mode effect.

8. Painting with a soft brush inside the masked area helps fine-tune the masked edge (see "Painting in Layer Masks" later in this chapter for more about the technique).

Note: The accompanying CD-ROM includes a video lesson on filling selections in a layer mask.

Feathering Layer Masks

Photoshop Elements also allows you to feather (or blur) a selection in a grouped layer mask. In Chapter 3, "Modifying Selections," you saw that applying a feather to a selection adds a soft edge to it. This can be extremely helpful when combining image layers, as it allows you to create a much more realistic blend. It makes the edges between layers less conspicuous. When applying a feathered edge to a selection in a layer mask, you can use either the pre- or post-feathering techniques described in Chapter 3. However, you may find that pre-feathering (when applicable) saves you a step.

For example, here's how I used a feathered selection to mask one photograph inside another when creating the "Big Apple" composite:

1. I selected the intended mask area using the Selection Brush (see Chapter 2) and then softened the selection edge by applying a feather amount of 10 pixels (see Chapter 3 for more detail on this "pre-feathering" technique).

2. To create a Levels adjustment layer, I clicked the Adjustment Layer icon and selected Levels from the pop-up menu. In the Levels dialog that appeared, I made no adjustments and simply clicked OK. Elements automatically filled the feathered selection with black in the Levels adjustment layer mask, as evidenced by the layer thumbnail.

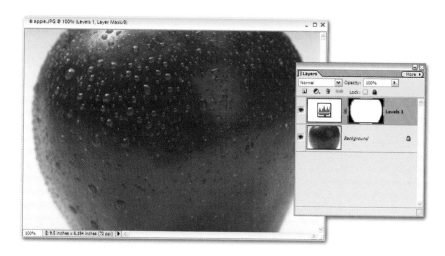

3. I dragged and dropped the New York City image into the document (see Chapter 4), and positioned it above the Levels adjustment layer containing the feathered mask.

4. Pressing Ctrl+Shift+U (Win) or ⌘+Shift+G (Mac) then desaturated the image. To add some roundness to the NYC image, I applied the Spherize filter by choosing Filter > Distort > Spherize (for more on filters, see Chapter 8).

To create a new group, I Alt/Option-clicked between the new Levels adjustment layer and the NYC image layer above it in the Layers palette.

6. I changed the NYC layer blend mode to Soft Light and renamed the layer "NYC 100% soft light." Changing the blend mode to Soft Light allows you to see through the NYC image to the apple underneath. All white areas are dropped out.

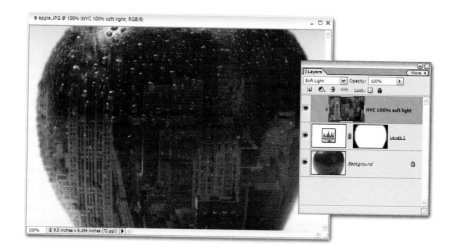

7. After duplicating the NYC image layer and applying several adjustment layers and various blend modes, the big apple image takes on this final form (for more detail on these stages, see the example "Interactive Blend Modes" in Chapter 5, "The Power of Opacity and Blending").

Note: As an alternative to feathering, you can also apply any of the available blur filters (Gaussian, Motion, Radial, etc.) to a pixel-based layer mask.

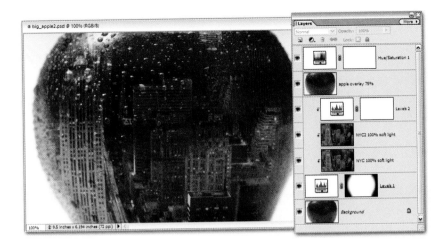

Gradient Blending with Layer Masks

By definition, a gradient is a continuous transition of colors. Gradients in Elements can contain a transition that blends from black to white, from one color to another, or contain an entire series of colors (see Figure 6.5). Gradients can also blend from opaque colors to transparent, a technique that is commonly used when blending images using layer masks.

Figure 6.5

Top: Gradients can blend from black to white, from one color to another, or contain an entire series of colors. Bottom: Opacity gradients blend from one opacity level to another. These types of gradients allow you to see through them, as shown here.

Before we begin learning how to apply gradients in layer masks, let's first take a close look at Photoshop Elements' Gradient tool, the available gradient presets, and the Gradient Editor.

The Gradient Tool

The Gradient tool allows you to apply a chosen gradient by clicking and dragging in any direction. You can access the tool by clicking the Gradient tool icon in the Tools palette or by pressing G on your keyboard.

     To use the Gradient tool, select a layer or layer mask in the Layers palette, choose a preset gradient from the Gradient Picker, and click and drag in any direction. Your initial click point determines where the first color of the gradient begins, and the point where you release the mouse button determines where the last color of the gradient ends. To help you visualize the transition, Elements displays a crosshair icon at either end of the line drawn with the tool (see Figure 6.6). The gradient appears in the image immediately after you let up on the mouse button.

—The Gradient Tool

Figure 6.6

Top: As you click and drag with the Gradient tool, Elements displays a line with a crosshair positioned at either end. Bottom: Once you release the mouse, Elements applies the gradient. Shown here is an opacity gradient applied to a grouped layer mask, which creates the "see-through" effect.

Note: Holding down Shift as you click and drag with the Gradient tool allows you to constrain the applied gradient to 45° angles.

The Gradient tool also has its own set of options in the options bar. You'll find a gradient preset menu, an Edit button that launches the Gradient Editor dialog, and several buttons for choosing a type of gradient to apply. Each gradient type is represented in the options bar by a descriptive icon, including Linear, Radial, Angle, Reflected, and Diamond.

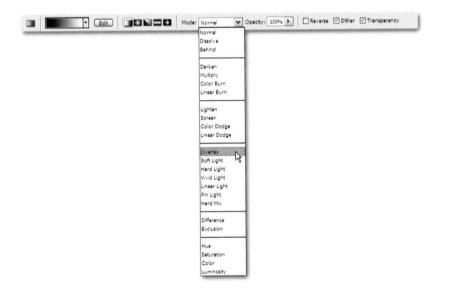

The options bar also allows you to apply a specific blend mode to gradients applied with the gradient tool. To use this option, you must choose the blend mode from the options bar menu before clicking and dragging with the tool. The blend mode options available in the options bar menu are the same ones you'll find in the Layers palette blend mode menu. Next to the blend mode list is an opacity field, where you can enter an opacity value. You must enter this value before you apply the gradient with the tool.

Navigating the Blend Modes

Once you've selected the Gradient tool (or any tool containing blend mode options), you can scroll through the options bar blend mode list by pressing Shift+ (to go forward) and Shift- (to go backward). Note that whenever a tool that does not contain blend mode options is selected (such as the Move tool), Shift+ and Shift- changes the blend mode for the currently selected layer.

Enabling the Reverse option switches the order of colors in the gradient. Enabling the Dither option creates a smoother blend between colors and prevents any banding (noticeable lines that appear in the gradient blend) from occurring. Enabling the Transparency option tells Elements to apply the gradient's transparency mask should the chosen gradient contain transparency. As a general rule, you should keep the Dither and Transparency options selected at all times.

Gradient Presets

To access the available gradient presets, click the down arrow next to the currently selected gradient thumbnail in the options bar. Doing so reveals the Gradient Picker. By default, the Gradient Picker displays the default set of gradients in a list of small thumbnails. With tooltips enabled, hovering over each thumbnail in the menu reveals the gradient preset name. You can resize the picker by clicking the bottom-left corner of the window and dragging out.

Renaming a Gradient

If you've made some adjustments to a gradient, it makes sense to rename it to something more descriptive that reflects those changes. You can rename a selected gradient by right-clicking (Win) or Control-clicking (Mac) and choosing Rename Gradient from the contextual menu.

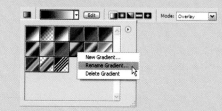

Enter a new name in the Gradient Name dialog that appears and click OK.

To change the way the gradient presets are displayed, click the menu button to reveal the flyout window. Here you can choose to display the gradient presets as small or large thumbnails, in small or large list view, or as text only (see Figure 6.7).

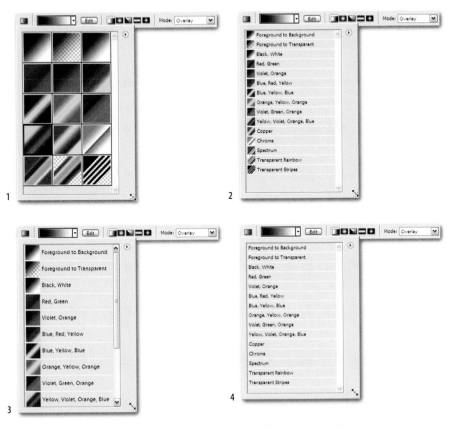

Figure 6.7 Modifying the Gradient Editor display of presets (1) Large Thumbnail view; (2) Small List View; (3) Large List View; (4) Text Only View

The bottom portion of the flyout menu contains a list of available gradient sets (also referred to as libraries). From this list you can choose which set of gradients to display in the menu window (see Figure 6.8). The sets are categorized by appearance, such as the Pastels set, which contains gradients using only pastel colors, or the Metals set, which contains gradients that emulate the color of reflected metal surfaces. Every time a new set is chosen, it replaces the currently visible set in the menu list. You can only view one set at a time.

Figure 6.8

The flyout menu gives you access to all of the available gradient presets. Shown here is the Metals set.

You can delete a selected gradient by right-clicking (Win) or Control-clicking (Mac) and choosing Delete Gradient from the contextual menu. Elements removes it from the list immediately.

Deleted gradients can be restored by choosing Reset Gradients from the flyout menu. When resetting, you have the option to save any changes made to the gradient settings. To do so, click Save in the warning dialog that appears. Elements then displays the Save dialog where you can name the new set. The default file location on your system for custom presets is in the Program Files\Adobe\ Photoshop Elements 4.0\Presets \Gradients folder (Win) or Applications/Adobe Photoshop Elements 4.0/Presets/Gradients (Mac). If you choose not to save, all changes made to the gradient presets, including any added new presets, will be lost.

CHAPTER 6: COMPOSITING WITH MASKS

Navigating the Presets

Press Shift+comma to select the first preset in the category list. Press Shift+period to select the last preset in the list. To scroll forward through the list, press the period key. To scroll backward, press the comma key.

The Gradient Editor

To enable you to edit existing gradients or create new ones, Photoshop Elements provides the Gradient Editor (see Figure 6.9). To access the editor, select a gradient from the Gradient Picker and click the Edit button, or click the gradient thumbnail in the options bar.

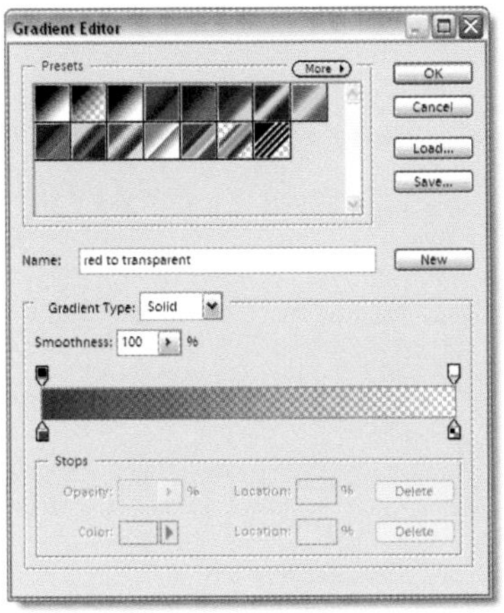

Figure 6.9
The Gradient Editor dialog allows you to modify and create gradients.

To edit an existing gradient, select a preset from the menu at the top of the editor dialog. You can load any of the available gradient sets in the window by clicking the More button and choosing a different set from the flyout menu. Just as you can with the preset menu, you can also change the Editor's preset display. From the flyout menu, select small or large thumbnails, small or large list view, or text only (see Figure 6.10).

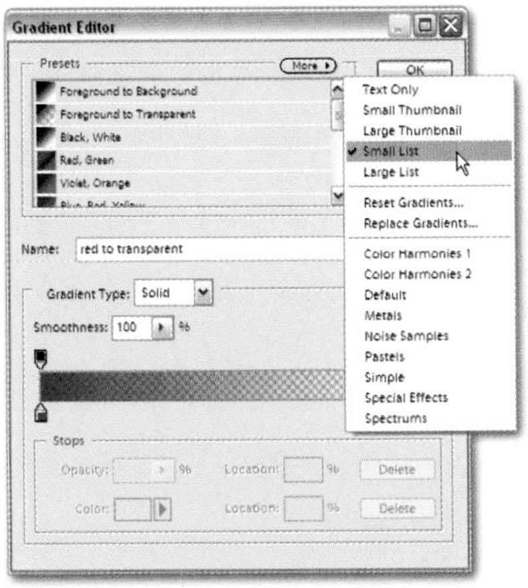

Figure 6.10
You can change the Gradient Editor preset display by choosing an option from the flyout menu.

Once a preset is selected, you can alter the gradient blend by doing any of the following:

- Drag any of the color stops under the gradient bar to the left or right.
- Add color stops by clicking anywhere under the gradient bar.
- Delete a color from the gradient by dragging its color stop off the editor window, or select the color stop and then click the Delete button at the bottom of the dialog.

Note: You must always have at least two colors present in a traditional solid-color gradient. Opacity gradients can contain one or more opacity levels and colors.

The controls located at the bottom of the editor dialog allow you to change the color of a selected color stop. Click the color swatch to access the Color Picker and choose a new color (see Figure 6.11). Click the arrow next to the swatch to access a pop-up menu and apply the Foreground, Background, or User color.

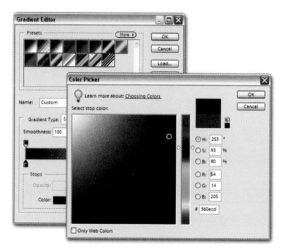

Figure 6.11

Use the Color Picker to change the color of a selected gradient color stop.

Select any of the opacity stops above the gradient bar to apply different opacity values to the gradient blend. With an opacity stop selected, enter a new opacity value in the opacity field at the bottom of the dialog (see Figure 6.12). You can add, delete, and reposition opacity stops using the same methods you use with color stops.

When all of your adjustments have been made, enter a name for the gradient in the Name field, and click the New button to add your custom preset to the set. The new gradient preset appears at the end of the menu list.

Figure 6.12
You can adjust the opacity of a gradient by selecting an opacity stop and entering a value in the field below.

Example: A Wedding Collage, Part 1

Now that you've been introduced to the tools for working with gradients in Photoshop Elements, let's take a look at how we can use them along with layer masks to combine images.

This example shows how I used layer masks and gradients to blend image layers in the wedding montage that first appeared in Chapter 1.

1. With the chosen background image open, I opened a second wedding image, selected it, and then imported via drag-and-drop (see Chapter 4). The imported image appears on its own layer above the Background layer, and I used the Move tool to position it in the upper-left corner of the document. Finally, I renamed the layer "book/rings."

2. To activate the Background layer in the Layers palette, I pressed Alt/Opt+[(left bracket). I added a Levels adjustment layer by clicking the Adjustment layer icon and selecting Levels from the pop-up menu. As usual, I made no adjustments and simply closed the dialog by clicking OK. I created a new group by Alt/Option-clicking between the new Levels adjustment layer and the book/rings layer above it in the Layers palette.

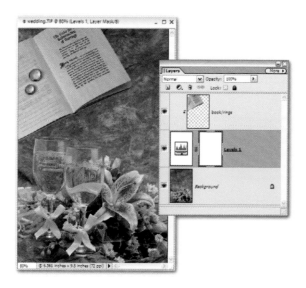

3. On my keyboard, I pressed the letter G to access the Gradient tool. In the options bar, I selected the Foreground to Transparent preset from the Gradient Picker. I then pressed D to reset the application default colors back to black foreground and white background. I set the Gradient tool opacity to 50% by pressing 5 on the keyboard. With the tool settings ready to apply, I went to the document window and drew a line from the bottom-right corner of the book image to the center of the book spine.

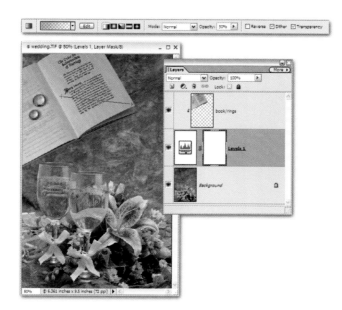

4. I pressed Alt/Opt+] (right bracket) to activate the book/rings layer and then reduced the layer's opacity level to 80%.

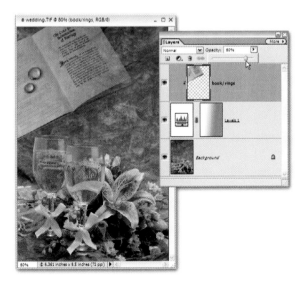

The remaining steps to complete this collage require the use of the Brush tool. Before we jump into painting in layer masks, let's take a look at the Brush tool and its various options. We'll complete this project at the end of the next section.

Note: The accompanying CD-ROM includes a video lesson on using gradients with layer masks.

Painting in Layer Masks

Painting in layer masks with the Brush tool is the best hands-on technique for combining images in Photoshop Elements. This method gives you the most control, and it is completely nondestructive. No pixels harmed!

Before we get started with painting in layer masks, let's take a close look at the Brush tool, the available brush presets, and additional brush options that allow you to create and save presets of your own.

The Brush Tool

The Brush tool allows you to paint with pixels in Photoshop Elements. You can access the tool by clicking the Brush tool icon in the Tools palette or by pressing the letter B on your keyboard.

To use the Brush tool, select a layer or layer mask in the Layers palette, then choose a brush from the preset list and click and drag in any direction. The brush behaves just like a traditional paintbrush. To help guide your brush stroke, Elements displays a circle icon that follows your mouse as you paint with the tool. The brush stroke appears onscreen in real time as you paint (see Figure 6.13).

Holding down Shift as you click and drag with the Brush tool allows you to constrain the applied brush stroke to 90° angles. To create a straight line at any angle with the brush, click to designate the start point and Shift-click to designate the end point.

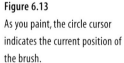

Figure 6.13
As you paint, the circle cursor indicates the current position of the brush.

The Brush tool also has its own set of options in the options bar, including a brush preset menu, size and opacity controls, a Mode menu, and airbrush capabilities (see Figure 6.14). The options bar also includes Tablet Options, for working with a graphics pen and tablet (see the sidebar) and More Options (as discussed in "Customizing and Creating Brushes" later in the chapter, these allow you to edit or create brush presets). The list of blend mode options available in the options bar's Mode menu are the same as in the Layers palette blend mode menu. To use these options, you must choose them from the options bar before painting with the tool.

Note: You can also increase or decrease the brush size in 10-pixel increments as you paint by pressing the bracket keys. Press] to increase and [to decrease.

Brush Preset Menu   Airbrush Capabilities

Figure 6.14 The Brush tool options

Display and Cursor Preferences for Brush Tips

Photoshop Elements 4 contains two new Display & Cursor preference options, both of which apply to the Brush tool. To access the Display & Cursors panel, choose Edit > Preferences > Display & Cursors (Win) or Photoshop Elements > Preferences > Displays & Cursors (Mac).

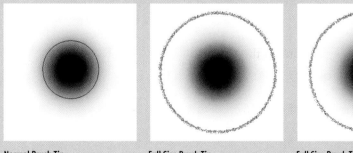

Full Size Brush Tip Enabling this option causes the circle cursor to reflect the edge of the brush, where the brush will stop affecting the image, whereas Normal Brush Tip (the default setting) displays the halfway point at which the color will disappear gradually.

Show Crosshair in Brush Tip Enabling this option causes a small crosshair to appear in the center of the circle brush cursor. This can be especially useful when using the Full Size Brush Tip option, because it can help you visualize exactly where the center of the brush is when painting with such a large cursor.

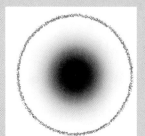

Normal Brush Tip   Full Size Brush Tip   Full Size Brush Tip with Crosshair

167

BLENDING WITH MASKS AND GROUPS

Tablet Options

To get the realistic look and feel of a traditional paintbrush, you should consider using a graphics pen and tablet. Elements contains Tablet Options that allow you to take advantage of graphics tablet pressure sensitivity.

With these options enabled, you can let the applied pressure of the pen control the size, opacity, roundness, hue jitter, or scatter of the brush stroke. Note that these settings must be enabled under More Options in the options bar in order to control them with pressure sensitivity.

No Tablet Options Enabled   Size, Opacity, and Roundness   With Hue Jitter and Scatter Options Enabled
                                   Options Enabled

Brush Presets

The Brush tool in Photoshop Elements ships with an entire library of presets. In addition, you can customize these presets and even create your own.

To access the available brush presets, click the down arrow next to the currently selected brush thumbnail in the options bar. Doing so reveals the brush preset menu. By default, the preset menu displays the default set of brushes in a list with a thumbnail that contains a sample stroke. With tooltips enabled, hovering the mouse over each thumbnail in the menu reveals the brush preset name. You can resize the menu by clicking and dragging out the bottom-left corner of the window.

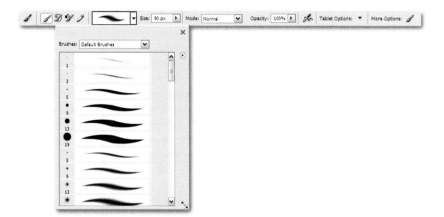

Renaming Brushes

If you've made some adjustments to a brush, it makes sense to rename it to something more descriptive that reflects those changes. You can rename a selected brush by right-clicking (Win) or Control-clicking (Mac) and choosing Rename Brush from the contextual menu.

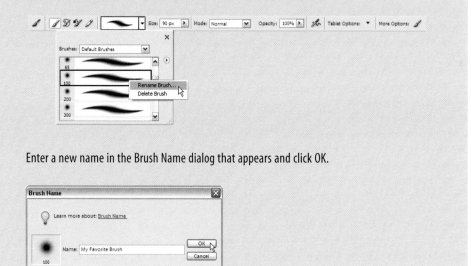

Enter a new name in the Brush Name dialog that appears and click OK.

To change the way the brush presets are displayed, click the menu button to reveal the flyout window. Here you can choose to display the brush presets as small or large thumbnails, in small or large list view, or as text only (see Figure 6.15).

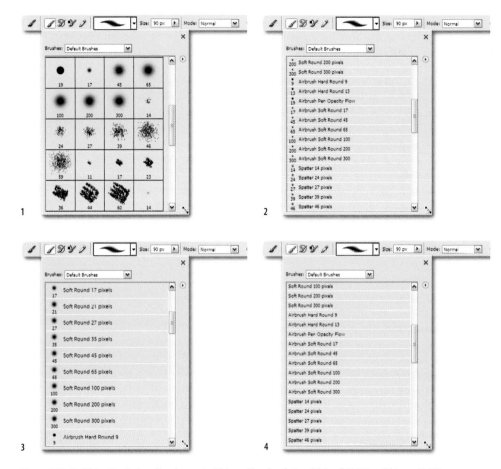

Figure 6.15 Modifying the display of brush presets: (1) Large Thumbnail view; (2) Small List View; (3) Large List View; (4) Text Only View

At the top of the preset window, the Brushes menu lets you select which of Elements' available brush libraries to display in the menu window (see Figure 6.16). Each new library you select will be displayed in the menu list until you replace it with another selection. You can only view one library at a time.

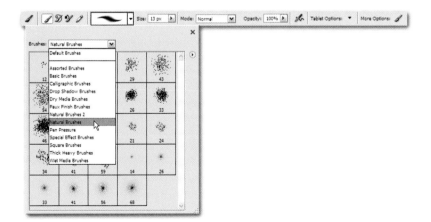

Figure 6.16 The Brushes menu gives you access to all of the available brush presets. Shown here is the Natural Brushes set.

You can delete a selected brush by right-clicking (Win) or Control-clicking (Mac) and choosing Delete Brush from the context menu. Elements removes it from the library list immediately.

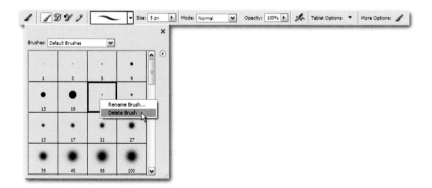

Fortunately, you can restore deleted brushes to the library by choosing Reset Brushes from the flyout menu. When deleting, a warning dialog appears to remind you that by doing so, you are changing the brush library. To commit to the change, click OK.

To save changes made to a library, choose Save Brushes from the flyout menu. Elements then displays the Save dialog, where you can name the new library. The default file location on your system for custom brush presets is in the Program Files\Adobe\Photoshop Elements 4.0\ Presets\ Brushes folder (Win) or Applications/Adobe Photoshop Elements 4.0/Presets/Brushes (Mac). If you choose not to save and proceed to apply the Reset Brushes command, all changes you've made to the brush presets will be lost.

The Preset Manager

Photoshop Elements contains presets for gradients, brushes, patterns, and swatches. Most often, you'll access these presets through the options bar when a related tool is selected. (The exception is swatches, which are accessible through the Color Swatches palette.) You can also add to or customize any of these sets using the Preset Manager.

The Preset Manager dialog is accessible under the Edit menu, or from the preset window (or Color Swatches palette) flyout menu. At the top of the dialog, choose a category (Brushes, Swatches, Gradients, or Patterns) from the Preset Type menu.

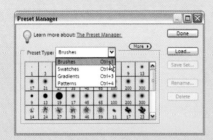

By default, the Preset Manager dialog displays the chosen set for all preset types in small thumbnail view. With tooltips enabled, hovering over each thumbnail in the menu reveals the preset name. To change the way the presets are displayed, click the More button to reveal the flyout window and choose a different view option (these vary depending on which preset type is selected). You can resize the dialog by clicking and dragging out the bottom-left corner of the window.

You can select a preset by clicking a thumbnail in the list. Shift-click to select multiple, contiguous presets; Ctrl/⌘-click to select multiple, noncontiguous presets. You can rename selected presets by clicking the Rename button, or delete them by clicking the Delete button.

The Preset Manager also allows you to save, load, and reset libraries. You can access any of these options from the flyout menu, just as you would from the options bar preset window.

Customizing and Creating Brushes

Photoshop Elements also allows you to edit existing brush presets or create new ones, using the Additional Brush Options dialog (see Figure 6.17). To access the dialog, select a brush from the preset menu and click the More Options button in the options bar.

Figure 6.17 The Additional Brush Options dialog allows you to modify and create brushes.

The Additional Brush Options dialog contains a series of controls that can alter the way a brush behaves. In Elements, these are called *brush dynamics*. As you make adjustments in the dialog, the brush thumbnail in the options bar dynamically changes to reflect your adjustments. You can adjust all of the settings except for Angle and Roundness either by using the scroll bar or by entering a value in the accompanying field. Here is a brief description of what each setting does:

Spacing: Controls the distance between marks in a brush stroke.

Normal Spacing

Increased Spacing

Fade: Sets the incremental rate (from 0 to 9999) for paint flow to fade to nothing. Lower values fade quicker. Smaller brushes generally require higher fade values.

Fade Setting of 40

Fade Setting of 60

Fade Setting of 80

Hue Jitter: Sets the rate at which the stroke color switches from the Foreground Color to the Background Color. Higher values produce more frequent switches.

Without Hue Jitter

With Hue Jitter

Hardness: Controls the hardness of the brush's center. The higher the value, the harder the stroke.

0% Hardness

100% Hardness

Scatter: Determines how brush marks are distributed in a stroke. Higher values increase the scattering area. Lower values result in denser strokes with less scattering.

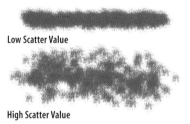

Low Scatter Value

High Scatter Value

Angle: Specifies the angle of offset for an elliptical brush's long axis. To adjust the angle, drag the arrowhead in the angle icon or enter a value in the field.

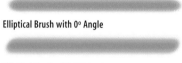

Elliptical Brush with 0° Angle

Elliptical Brush with 48° Angle

Roundness: Indicates the ratio between the short and long axis of a brush and ultimately affects the shape of a brush tip. To specify a roundness percentage, drag either dot in the angle icon closer to or further away from the center, or enter a value in the field. A value of 100% results in a circular brush; 0% results in a linear brush; all other values result in varying elliptical brushes.

0% Roundness

50% Roundness

100% Roundness

Note: To apply your customized dynamic brush settings to all brushes in Elements, check the Keep These Settings For All Brushes option located at the bottom of the Additional Brush Options dialog.

Example: A Wedding Collage, Part 2

Now that we have a better understanding of brushes, let's take a look at how we can use them along with layer masks to combine images. We can pick up where we left off with part 1 of this example tutorial.

1. With the layered document already open, I opened a third wedding image, this one of a bride, and imported it using drag-and-drop (see Chapter 4). The imported photo appeared on its own layer at the top of the layer stack, and I used the Move tool to position it in the upper-right corner of the document. Finally, I named the layer "bride."

2. I activated the book/rings layer underneath the bride layer in the Layers palette by pressing Alt/Opt+[(left bracket). Then, to gain access to a layer mask, I added a Levels adjustment layer by clicking the Adjustment layer icon and selecting Layers from the pop-up menu. I didn't make any adjustments and closed the dialog by clicking OK. By Alt/Option-clicking between the new Levels adjustment layer and the bride layer above it in the Layers palette, I created a new group.

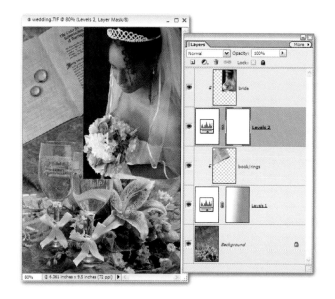

3. To access the Brush tool, I pressed the letter B on the keyboard. In the options bar, I chose the Default Brushes preset menu and then the Soft Round 65 pixel brush. I then pressed D to reset the application default colors back to black foreground and white background. In the document window, I masked out the area surrounding the bride by painting in the layer mask with the soft round brush.

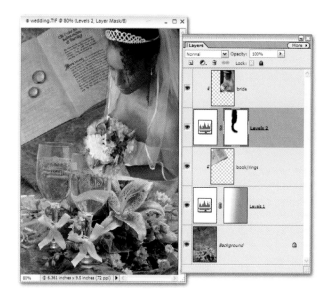

4. The result was close to what I wanted, but the bride still stood out too much from the background. So I pressed 3 to change the Brush tool opacity setting to 30% and painted around the edge of the bride image in the layer mask to make it slightly transparent. Having the Show Crosshair Tip Cursor display preference enabled made guiding the brush along the edge much easier. Any areas that are made too transparent by over-applying strokes with the brush can be fixed by pressing X to make white the foreground color, or by switching to the Eraser tool, selecting the same brush preset and brush opacity, and painting over the areas again. This is the beauty of nondestructive editing with layer masks!

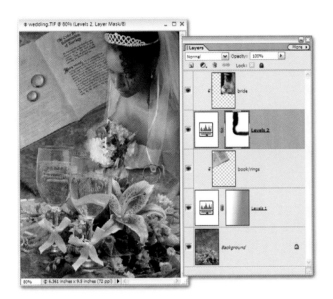

Note: The accompanying CD-ROM includes a video lesson on painting with brushes in layer masks.

Vector-Based Clipping Masks

One other way that you can combine images in a layered composition is to group image layers to vector-based shape or type layers. Doing so allows you to place an image within editable text characters or inside a custom shape, where it automatically crops to fit the characters or shape. If the text or shape needs to change, Elements will change the image cropping to match.

Type Masks

One of the most interesting and effective ways of making text and art work together is to fill the characters of large display type with an image, as illustrated in Figure 6.18. In Photoshop Elements, cropping an image inside editable text is easy. All you need to do is group the image layer to the type layer underneath it in the Layers palette. The great thing about type masks is that they allow you to edit the text, and thus change the crop area, at any time—without damaging any pixels! Let's take a step-by-step look at how this is done:

Figure 6.18

Top: Grouping an image layer to a type layer allows you to create unique combinations of text and art. Bottom: You can edit the text and maintain the crop of the image inside the characters. Here the text was italicized and the first letter capitalized.

1. Open the image that you'd like to place inside some type. In this example, the image of a cloudy blue sky is a good match for the "imagine" text. We associate the sky and the color blue with imagination, but a cloudless sky would simply look like blue type; we wouldn't recognize it as the sky.

   Double-click the Background layer to access the New Layer dialog. Enter a new name for the layer ("sky" in this example), and click OK. This converts the Background layer into an image layer.

www.photospin.com ©2005

2. To begin creating your text, press T to access the Horizontal Type tool. In the tool's options bar, select a bold face font with characters that are thick enough for an image placed within them to be recognizable, as well as a large point size, and an alignment option. In the example, I've chosen Haettenschweiler on the Windows platform, 282 pt, centered. Click in the center of the document window and type your text ("imagine" in the example). As soon as you begin typing, a new text layer is added to the document above the image layer.

3. Click the Move tool icon in the Tools palette and position the text accordingly. Notice that the name of the type layer in the Layers palette automatically displays what was typed. Press Ctrl/⌘+[(left bracket) to position the type layer underneath the image layer. The type will disappear in the document window because the opaque image layer above it in the palette now covers it up.

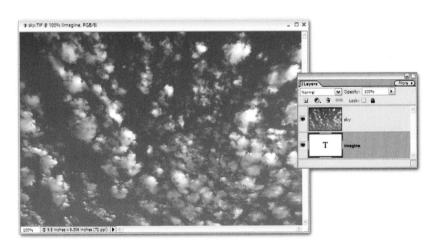

4. Create a group by Alt/Option-clicking between the type layer and the image layer above it in the Layers palette. The image will be automatically cropped inside the text characters. If you'd like to adjust which part of the image is visible, you can select the image layer and reposition it inside the letters with the Move tool.

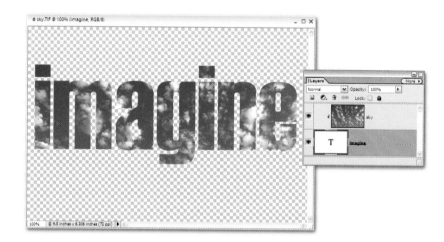

5. Now we need to create a background for the combined image. Select the type layer in the Layers palette and then Ctrl/⌘-click the Create New Layer button. Doing so creates a new layer underneath the type layer. If the application default colors are not currently set to black foreground and white background, press D to reset them. Then press Ctrl+Backspace (Win) or ⌘+Delete (Mac) to apply a white fill to the new layer. Rename the layer "white background."

6. To take the image one step further, select the type layer and apply a layer style to it. In the example shown here, the Wow - Plastic Aqua Blue style is applied (for more on styles, see Chapter 8).

Note: The accompanying CD-ROM includes a video lesson on combining type and art.

Shape Masks

Shape masks work pretty much like type masks; to create one, all you need to do to is group an image layer to the shape layer underneath it in the Layers palette. You can change the crop area nondestructively by transforming the shape. Figure 6.19 shows an example in which the outline of a butterfly is filled with an extreme close-up of its markings. Let's take a step-by-step look at how this image was created:

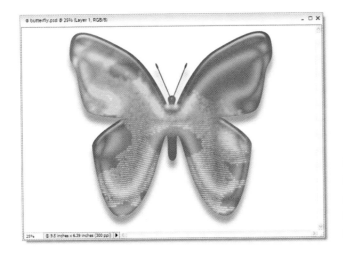

Figure 6.19
Grouping an image layer to a shape layer allows you to create unique combinations of shapes and photos.

1. Open the image that you'd like to put inside a shape. In this example, the image is a close-up of a butterfly wing. Press Ctrl+A (Win) or ⌘+A (Mac) to select the whole image; then press Ctrl+Shift+J (Win) or ⌘+Shift+J (Mac) to cut the selected image from the Background layer and place it on a new layer above in the Layers palette. Rename the layer accordingly ("butterfly 1" in this example).

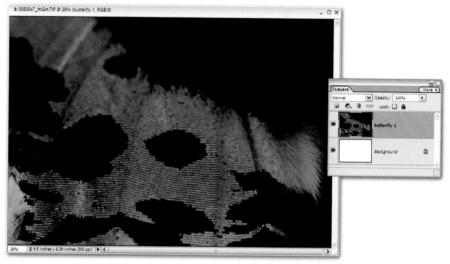

www.photospin.com ©2005

2. To create the shape, begin by pressing Alt/Opt+[(left bracket) to activate the Background layer. Then press U to access the Shape tool. In the Options bar, click the Custom Shape Tool icon and select a shape from the Custom Shape Picker (in this example, I selected butterfly 2 from the Default library). Click and drag in the document window to draw the shape. Hold down Shift as you click and drag to constrain horizontal and vertical proportions. As soon as you begin drawing with the tool, a new shape layer is added to the document above the Background layer.

 Note: Holding down the spacebar as you click and drag with the Shape tool allows you to move the shape in the document window as you draw it.

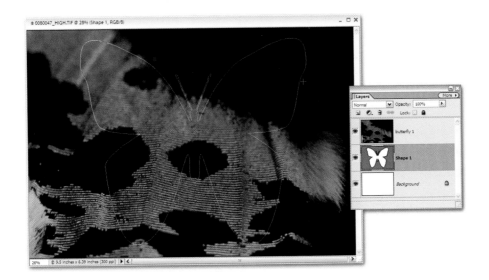

3. Create a group by Alt/Option-clicking between the Shape layer and the image layer above it in the Layers palette. The image is automatically cropped inside the shape. If you'd like to adjust the crop, you can select the image layer (e.g., butterfly 1) and reposition it inside the shape with the Move tool.

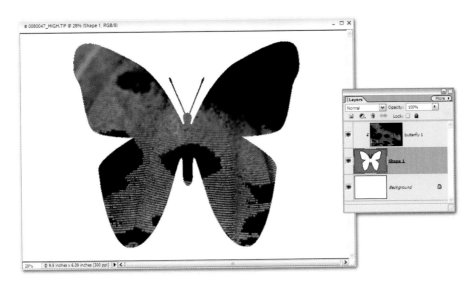

4. You can add some dimension to the Shape layer by applying a Layer Style to it. In the example shown here, the Wow - Plastic Red style is applied (for more on styles, see Chapter 8).

5. To blend the image layer above with the shape layer's applied layer style attributes, select the image layer in the Layers palette and change its blend mode to something other than Normal. In this example, the Linear Dodge blend mode works best. Also, in this example lowering the layer's opacity level to 75% helps to even out the color between the two layers.

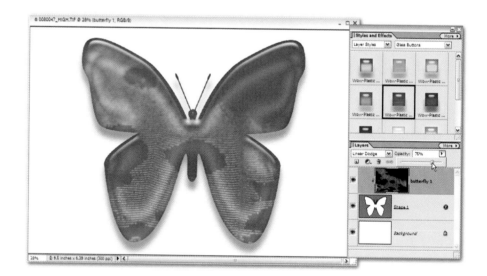

6. If you like, you can add a Hue and Saturation adjustment layer to the top of the layer stack and change the overall color of the image. In this example, I created a gold color by adjusting the Hue value to +22 , the Saturation to +29, and the Lightness to -6. Remember, applying a Hue and Saturation adjustment layer is a nondestructive way of altering color in a composition. These settings can be changed at any time without damaging any pixels.

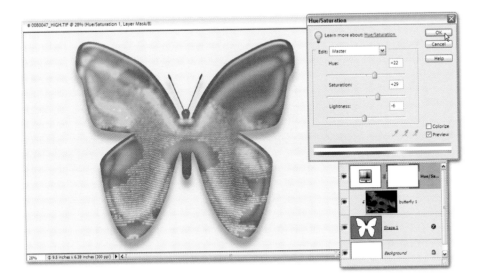

7. To keep the background area of the image white, we can fill a selection in the Hue and Saturation layer mask. Ctrl/CM-click the shape layer thumbnail in the Layers palette to make a selection of the shape, then press Ctrl+Shift+I (Win) or ⌘+Shift+I (Mac) to invert the selection. Click the Hue and Saturation adjustment layer in the palette and press Alt/Opt+Backspace to fill the inverted selection with black.

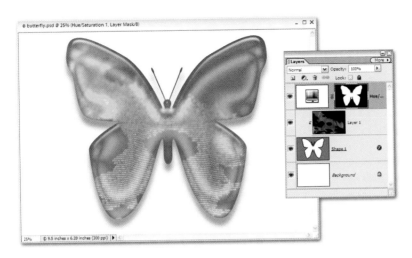

8. You can also import additional image layers and include them in the clipping group. In Figure 6.20, two more butterfly textures are added to the image. The new layers are named "butterfly 2" and "butterfly 3." The butterfly 2 layer blend mode is changed to Multiply, and the butterfly 3 layer blend mode is changed to Linear Dodge. You can view each of these grouped layers separately using the Layers palette visibility controls, or you can view them all at once to see the how the applied blend modes interact. The more you experiment, the more creative you can get!

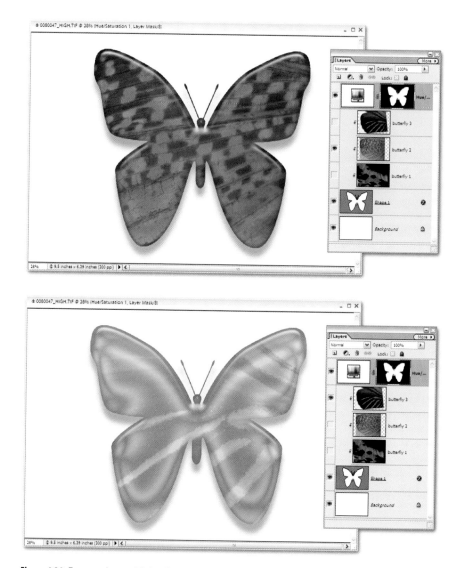

Figure 6.20 Two more layers added to the group: (top) the Butterfly 2 layer by itself; (bottom) the Butterfly 3 layer by itself.

Continued on next page

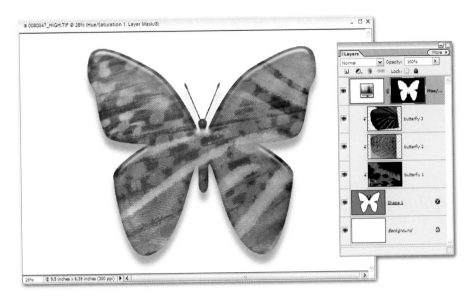

Figure 6.20 *(Continued)* All three texture layers visible at once.

Advanced Masking with Camera RAW

As you learned in the previous chapter, layer masks are an integral part of image compositing. By allowing you to edit image layers nondestructively, they provide you with maximum creative efficiency, and you should use them whenever possible. Using layer masks, you'll leave the original pixels unharmed so that you can make any subsequent image edits quickly and easily.

The techniques you've learned so far have all involved combining two or more different images, or an image and text. You can also use layers and layer masks to enhance a single image by combining differently edited versions of that image. This approach works well when—as often happens—different parts of an image need different corrections.

Chapter Contents
Working with Camera RAW Files
Combining Shadow/Highlight Information
Combining Color Temperature

The digital format that allows the most control over image correction is known as RAW, and the tool that Photoshop Elements provides for working with RAW files is the Camera RAW plug-in. In this chapter, we'll begin with a quick tutorial in using the plug-in, and then take a look at how to use layer masks with Camera RAW files to combine enhanced shadow/highlight information and color temperature adjustments.

Working with Camera RAW Files

One way to get the most out of image editing in Photoshop Elements is to work with Camera RAW files using the Camera RAW plug-in. This tool offers fine-tuning options that can't be made directly in the Elements workspace. As long as the photos you've chosen to work with are saved in the RAW format, you can edit them in 16-bit using the plug-in (perhaps saving different versions of the same image with different corrections), then open them in Elements, convert them to 8-bit, and combine them using layers and layer masks.

RAW Editing: 16-bit vs. 8-bit

There are many advantages to working with Camera RAW images, but what's the advantage of editing them in 16-bit? Well, 8-bit images contain up to 16.8 million colors, but 16-bit images contain up to 281 *trillion* colors. Therefore, editing RAW files in 16-bit with the plug-in greatly increases your color gamut. The disadvantage is that Elements does not allow you to use layers with 16-bit images, so you must open the edited RAW files in Elements and convert them to 8-bit before you can combine them.

In order to work with Camera RAW files in Elements, you must first have saved the images in the RAW format when you photographed them. All professional-level digital cameras, as well as most prosumer and many higher-end consumer cameras, allow you to save images in a native RAW file format (as well as in JPEG or TIFF format). Be sure to check your user guide to find out if your camera has this option. If so, you can usually choose it from the camera's setup menu.

Note: TIFF is not the same as RAW. TIFF files are not made up of raw image data, and therefore cannot be edited using the Photoshop Elements camera RAW plug-in.

Defining Camera RAW

When you shoot in JPEG format (or TIFF), the camera does some processing as it saves the image, including adding compression. RAW files are actually made up of unprocessed data just as it is captured by the camera's image sensor. Shooting in RAW format allows you to capture a wider range of colors and acquire much more accurate image detail. The downside is that the file size of a RAW image is much larger than a JPEG or TIFF because of all the extra information that is stored in the file. To accommodate this, you may need to purchase a media card with increased storage capacity, or invest in an extra hard drive.

Different cameras produce different types of RAW files, with different file extensions. For example, a RAW image captured by an Olympus digital camera has the .ORF file extension, while a RAW image captured by a Nikon camera has the .NEF extension. There are also RAW formats for Canon (.CRW), Minolta (.MRW), and Fuji (.RAF).

The Photoshop Elements Camera RAW plug-in can recognize most of these RAW file formats. For a current list of supported cameras and file types, along with installation instructions for the plug-in, refer to Adobe's website (www.adobe.com/support), and search for "supported cameras" (see Figure 7.1).

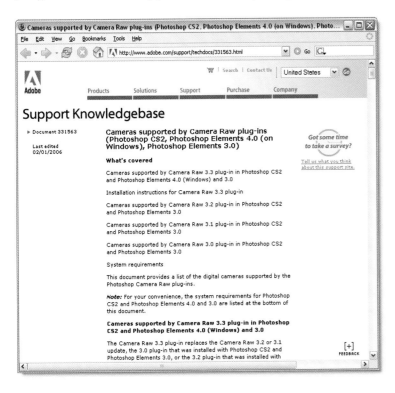

Figure 7.1

Refer to Adobe's website for an updated list of cameras and RAW file formats that Camera RAW supports.

DNG (Digital Negative) Format

In an attempt to standardize a format for all RAW images, Adobe has created the DNG (Digital Negative) format. Unfortunately, many camera manufacturers have not yet embraced this file format as Adobe had hoped they would. However, you can download and use Adobe's free Digital Negative Converter software, which allows you to convert RAW images into the more universal DNG format. The DNG Converter is available at www.adobe.com/products/dng.

The Camera RAW Dialog

Any time you open a RAW file in Elements, using either the File > Open command or by double-clicking the image thumbnail in the Organizer (Windows) or Bridge (Mac), the image is automatically displayed in the Camera RAW dialog. The RAW workspace allows you to edit the image's raw data by altering its white balance and exposure settings. You can also use this dialog to adjust the RAW image's shadow areas, brightness, contrast, and saturation (see Figure 7.2). On its Detail tab, you can adjust the sharpness, luminance, and color noise values (see Figure 7.3). You cannot access any of the traditional Elements tools or menus while the Camera RAW plug-in workspace is active.

Whenever you open a RAW file in the plug-in workspace, it always displays the most recently applied settings for that image. Any adjustments made with the plug-in are stored in the RAW file along with the image's original camera settings. This means that no matter what adjustments you've made using the plug-in, you can always revert to the original "as shot" settings at any time.

Zoom   Hand   White Balance   Rotate Image 90°   Rotate Image 90°   Preview   Shadow Clipping   Highlight Clipping
Tool   Tool   Tool   Counterclockwise   Clockwise   Option   Warning Option   Warning Option

RGB Values for
Current Cursor
Position in the
Image Preview

Histogram

Settings Menu

White Balance
Controls

Tonal
Controls

Depth   Zoom   Image
Menu   Controls   Preview

Figure 7.2 The Camera Raw plug-in workspace, with the Adjust tab visible

Figure 7.3 The Detail tab of the Camera Raw workspace

Camera RAW Settings

As you can see from Figures 7.2 and 7.3, the Camera RAW plug-in workspace contains many options for optimizing RAW images. Before we start optimizing and combining RAW images in Elements, let's first take a close look at the dialog and its various controls:

Image preview and navigation tools   The Camera Raw interface contains its own preview window and its own set of navigational controls, including a Zoom tool, a Zoom Level menu, a Hand tool, a clockwise rotation tool, and a counterclockwise rotation tool. The Preview window takes up the entire left side of the dialog, and the tools are positioned just above it in the upper left.

You can access the Zoom tool by pressing Z on the keyboard or by clicking the zoom tool icon. It works like the traditional Elements Zoom tool; you zoom in by clicking anywhere in the image preview area and zoom out by Alt/Option-clicking. You can also zoom in or out using the + or - zoom level buttons located underneath the image preview at the bottom left of the dialog. Or if you prefer, you can also choose a zoom level preset from the menu to the right of the + or - button. If you're accustomed to using the traditional zoom commands of Ctrl+ or - (Win) or ⌘+ or - (Mac), you can also use them in the RAW workspace environment. Finally, the Ctrl/Command and Alt/Option keys will temporarily change the current tool to the Zoom In and Zoom Out tools, respectively.

The Hand tool allows you to reposition a zoomed image in the window by clicking and dragging in the preview area. To access the tool, click the Hand icon or press H. You can also press and hold the spacebar to temporarily access the Hand tool while you have one of the other tools selected.

The Camera RAW workspace also offers two Rotate tools: one for rotating an image 90° clockwise and one for rotating 90° counterclockwise. You can change image orientation using either of these Rotate tools (see Figure 7.4). When you exit the camera RAW interface, the image's current orientation is saved along with the file and is displayed exactly the same way when reopened.

Depth menu   From this menu, you can choose whether to edit the raw image data in 8-bit/channel or 16-bit/channel.

Histogram and clipping tools   The Camera RAW workspace also contains its own histogram, positioned in the upper right of the dialog. It is similar to working with the Histogram palette when all color channels are made visible. The RAW histogram maps out all of the tonal values for the Red, Green, and Blue channels of the image, as well as the Cyan, Magenta, Yellow, and Black channels (Black is represented by the white area of the histogram). The histogram changes to reflect adjustments made to the image using the white balance and tonal controls.

Keep an eye on the histogram as you make your adjustments. In theory, a well-distributed histogram indicates an ideally exposed image. Clumps of color positioned to the far left or far right indicate that the image is either too dark or too light, respectively. If any one color is dominant, this indicates a color shift in that direction, which may or may not need to be adjusted, depending on the type of image you are working with.

You can use the Highlight And Shadow clipping controls along with the Histogram to help locate areas of the image that contain what is know as "clipping"—pixel values that are too bright or too dark to be represented. When the Clipping Warning options are enabled, the plug-in displays any areas containing highlights with no pixels (a.k.a blowout) in red, and any shadow areas containing pure black (a.k.a. blocked shadows) in blue (see Figure 7.5). Once you've identified clipped areas of an image, you can correct them using the tonal controls.

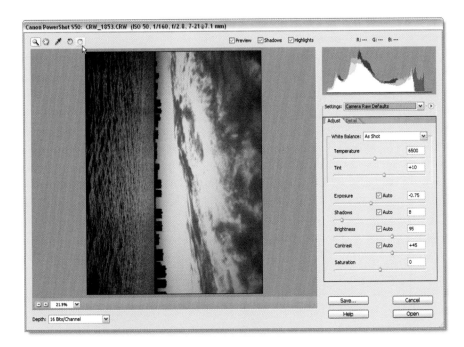

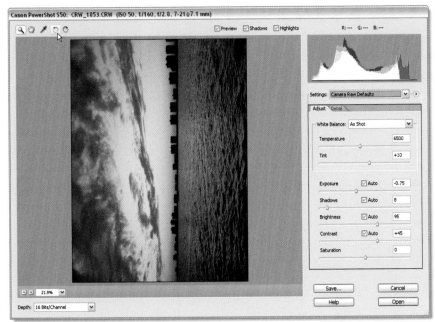

Figure 7.4 Rotating an image with the Rotate tools: (top) 90° clockwise; (bottom) 90° counterclockwise

Figure 7.5 With the Clipping Warning options enabled, highlight blowouts appear red and blocked shadows appear blue. Notice the clumps of color to the far right and left of the histogram. These also indicate that highlight and shadow clipping has occurred.

How to Read a Histogram

A histogram in Elements is a type of bar graph; the Levels dialog we've used in earlier chapters is an example. It contains 256 bars that vary in width and height to show the distribution of colors or tonal information in an image. Each bar represents one brightness value from black (on the far left) to white (on the far right). The height of each bar represents the number of pixels that correspond to that brightness value. The histogram helps you "see into" the image and locate where the darkest colors begin in each color channel and where the lightest colors end.

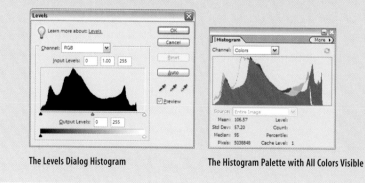

The Levels Dialog Histogram

The Histogram Palette with All Colors Visible

Settings menu Allows you to select from preset, custom, or previously used plug-in settings:

Image Settings applies the settings from the previous conversion of the image that you are currently working with. If the image has never been converted, then this is the same as choosing Camera RAW Defaults.

Camera RAW Defaults applies the default settings that you've created. If you haven't created your own default settings, then choosing this option applies the exposure, white balance, and sharpness settings as they were shot by the camera.

Previous Conversion applies the settings from the previous camera RAW image converted.

Custom is automatically selected anytime you move the white balance or tonal control sliders. You can save your custom settings as a new Camera RAW default by clicking the arrow to the right of the Settings menu and choosing Save New Camera RAW Defaults. To revert back to the original camera settings, choose Reset Camera RAW defaults.

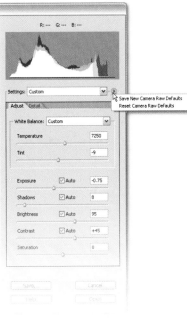

The Adjust Tab

Here is a brief description of the controls available in the Adjust tab of the Camera RAW dialog:

White Balance controls These settings allow you to adjust the temperature and tint of an image by choosing a preset lighting condition from the White Balance menu, or adjusting the settings manually with the Temperature and Tint controls. The preset menu includes the following options:

As Shot applies the camera's chosen white balance settings at the time of exposure.

Auto attempts to balance the temperature and tint of the image automatically.

Daylight adjusts the temperature and tint to reflect normal (or neutral) lighting conditions (5500 degrees Kelvin).

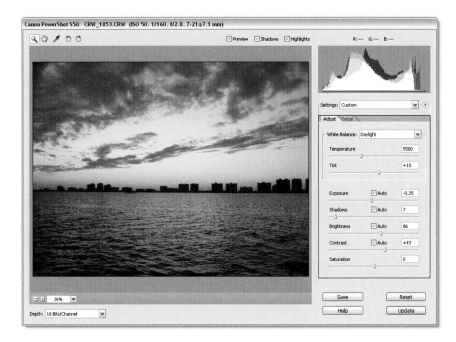

Cloudy adjusts the temperature and tint to reflect cool (or overcast) lighting conditions (6500 degrees Kelvin). For the sunset image, these settings are the same as As Shot.

Shade adjusts the temperature and tint to reflect cool light, full shade lighting conditions (7500 degrees Kelvin).

Tungsten adjusts the temperature and tint to reflect balanced tungsten lighting conditions (2850 degrees Kelvin). The name refers to incandescent electric lamps, whose filaments are made of tungsten.

Fluorescent adjusts the temperature and tint to reflect fluorescent lighting conditions, usually containing a green cast (3800 degrees Kelvin).

Flash adjusts the temperature and tint to reflect balanced lighting conditions as produced by the use of a camera flash (5500 degrees Kelvin, the same as Daylight).

Custom balances the image based on the settings applied manually with the Temperature and Tint controls. Moving the Temperature slider to the left makes colors appear cooler (or more blue); moving it to the right makes colors appear warmer (or more yellow). Moving the Tint slider to the left applies negative values, and adds green to the image; moving it to the right adds positive values, and adds magenta (see Figure 7.6).

Figure 7.6 Adjusting color temperature and tint manually. (1) Moving the Temperature slider to the left makes colors appear cooler (or more blue); (2) moving it to the right makes colors appear warmer (or more yellow).

Continued on next page

Figure 7.6 *(Continued)* (3) moving the Tint slider to the left applies negative values, and adds green to the image; and (4) moving it to the right adds positive values, and adds magenta.

Tonal controls Below the Temperature and Tint controls is a second group of sliders that allow you to apply tonal adjustments. To apply an automatic adjustment, leave the Auto check boxes above each slider selected. In most cases, these auto settings do a great job of adjusting the image; however, to apply a specific adjustment or create a certain effect, you can always adjust the image manually by moving the Exposure, Shadows, Brightness, Contrast, and Saturation sliders. Figures 7.7 through 7.11 illustrate the effects of increasing or decreasing the tonal controls.

Exposure: Moving the slider to the right increases the exposure, and as a result, lightens the image; moving it to the left decreases the exposure and darkens the image (Figure 7.7).

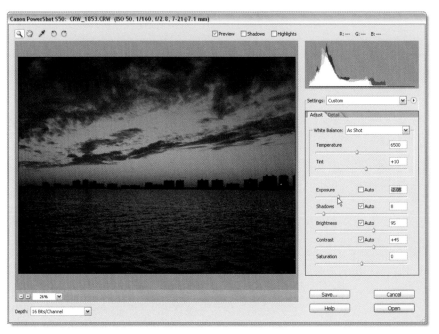

Figure 7.7 Top: Increasing the exposure lightens the image. Bottom: Decreasing the exposure darkens the image.

Shadows: Moving the slider to the right increases the density of the shadow areas, and as a result, darkens the image; moving it to the left lightens the shadow areas. Highlight areas are not affected by this adjustment (Figure 7.8).

Figure 7.8 Top: Increasing shadow density darkens the image. Bottom: Decreasing shadow density lightens it.

Brightness: This control is similar to the gamma slider located in the Levels dialog (the middle slider under the histogram) in that it can be used to adjust the mid-tones of an image; the only difference is that the Brightness slider redistributes the mid-tones using a linear adjustment. Moving the slider to the right lightens the image; moving it to the left darkens it (Figure 7.9).

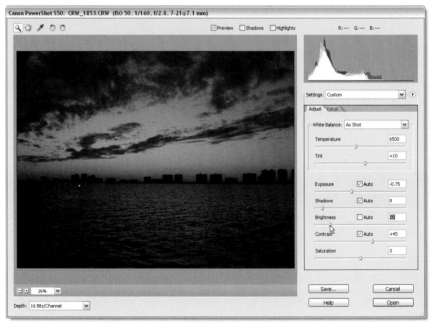

Figure 7.9 Top: Increasing brightness lightens an image. Bottom: Decreasing brightness darkens it.

Contrast: Moving the slider to the right expands the histogram to increase contrast between pixels; moving it to the left compresses the histogram to decrease contrast (Figure 7.10).

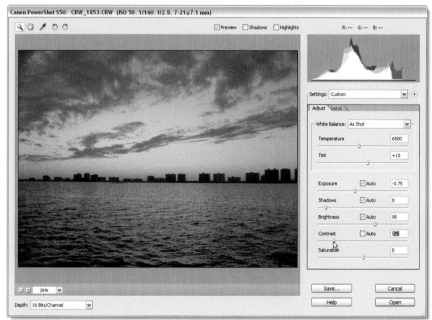

Figure 7.10 Top: Increasing contrast; Bottom: Decreasing contrast

Saturation: This control is similar to the Saturation slider located in Elements' Hue/Saturation dialog (the bottom slider) in that it can be used to adjust the strength, or color purity of the image. Moving the slider to the right increases saturation; moving it to the left decreases it (Figure 7.11).

Figure 7.11 Top: Increasing saturation; Bottom: Decreasing saturation

The Details Tab

On its Details tab, Camera Raw offers three controls that let you enhance sharpness, apply luminance smoothing, and reduce color noise. Figures 7.12 through 7.14 demonstrate their effects.

Sharpness This control is similar to applying the Unsharp Mask filter in Elements; it increases the amount of contrast between adjacent pixels. Unlike the Contrast slider, which affects the entire histogram, the Sharpness slider increases edge definition and creates the appearance of sharper focus. Moving the slider to the right increases the sharpening effect; moving it to the left decreases it (Figure 7.12).

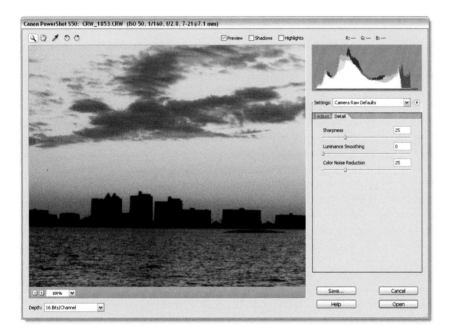

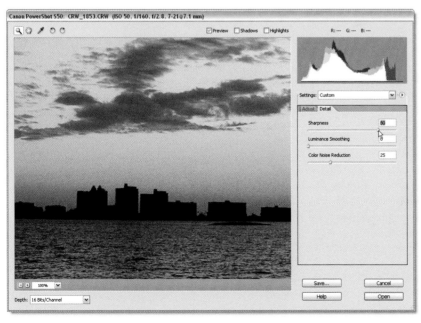

Figure 7.12 Top: An image with the default Sharpness setting; Bottom: the same image with increased sharpness

Note: Once opened, the Camera Raw plug-in automatically sharpens the image based on the camera model, the image ISO, and exposure settings. Any further sharpening with the Sharpness slider is a step usually best saved for last, especially when building a combined image project. In most cases, it's better to leave the plug-in Sharpness setting alone and not make any adjustments. Instead, use the Unsharp Mask filter after you've opened and combined the image in Elements (see Chapter 8).

Luminance Smoothing Oversharpening can cause random grayscale pixels (called noise) to appear in the image. Too much noise can make your image look grainy. To soften these areas of noise, you can apply a Luminance Smoothing adjustment. Moving the slider to the right increases the smoothing effect; moving it to the left decreases it (Figure 7.13).

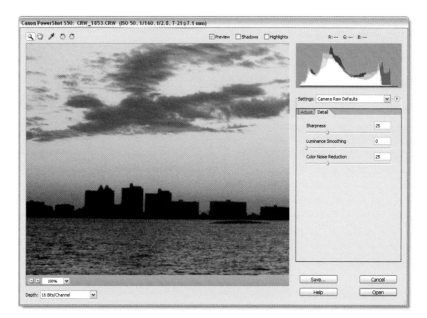

Figure 7.13 Top: Before luminance smoothing; Bottom: After luminance smoothing

Color Noise Reduction   Adjusting the Color Noise Reduction slider reduces the amount of random color pixels (or noise) that results from variations in image hue and saturation. Moving the slider to the right increases the amount of color noise reduction; moving it to the left decreases it (Figure 7.14).

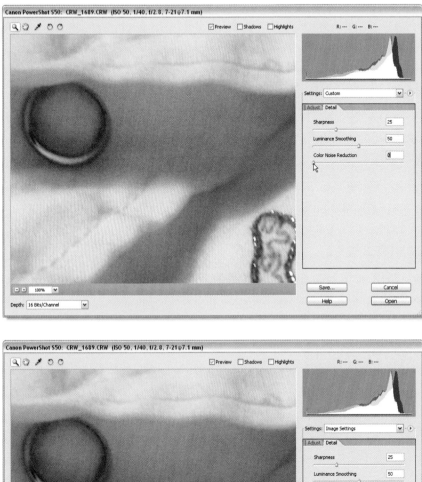

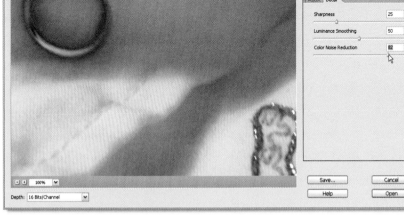

Figure 7.14 Top: Before color noise reduction; Bottom: After color noise reduction

Bypassing the Camera RAW Dialog

You can bypass the plug-in and open your RAW image directly into Elements by holding down Shift and double-clicking the image thumbnail in the Organizer (Win) or Bridge (Mac) file browser application. The plug-in always applies the most recently applied camera RAW settings for that image. If no adjustments have been made, it applies the Camera RAW default settings.

Combining Shadow/Highlight Information

Now that you're familiar with the Camera Raw plug-in and the tools it provides to edit RAW images, let's take a look at how we can fix common digital photography problems by creating different edited versions of a single RAW image and combining them in a layered composition.

Shooting in full sunlight, we often get areas of over- and underexposure in the same image. To fix this, you need to open a RAW file with the plug-in and then create two versions of the same image: one where you adjust the shadow information, and one where you adjust the highlight information. You can then convert both images to 8-bit mode and combine them using layers and layer masks.

The following example shows how I used the Camera Raw plug-in, along with layers and layer masks, to improve the photograph shown in Figure 7.15, where the mountains in the background are a little washed out and the shadows in the foreground are too deep, by fixing the shadow and highlight information on different layers and combining them. Figure 7.16 shows the result.

Figure 7.15
Parts of this photograph are overexposed, and parts are underexposed.

Figure 7.16
Using Camera RAW I corrected both problems in separate versions of the image, which I then combined in Elements using layers and layer masks.

1. Using the Organizer (Win) or Bridge (Mac) file browser application, I located the RAW image, and opened it in the Camera RAW workspace by double-clicking its thumbnail. No previous adjustments were made, so I started out working with the As Shot camera default settings. I made sure to change the Depth setting in the lower-left corner of the dialog to 16 bits/channel in order to ensure that I was working with the widest possible color gamut.

2. Next I used the sliders in the Adjust tab of the dialog to enhance the shadow information of the background mountain area of the photo. This was done by lowering the Exposure setting (moving the slider to the left), raising the Shadows setting (moving the slider right), and increasing the Contrast (moving the slider to the far right). With the Shadow clipping option enabled, I could see by the blue areas displayed in the Preview window that the clipped shadows were all located in the forefront bushes of the photograph, but not in the mountains. This was okay, because in this edited version of the RAW image I was only correcting the mountains; foreground shadows would be fixed separately. With the shadow information enhanced, I clicked Open to exit the plug-in dialog and open the image in the Elements workspace. I then chose File > Save As, renamed the image "mountains," and saved it as a PSD file (Photoshop document).

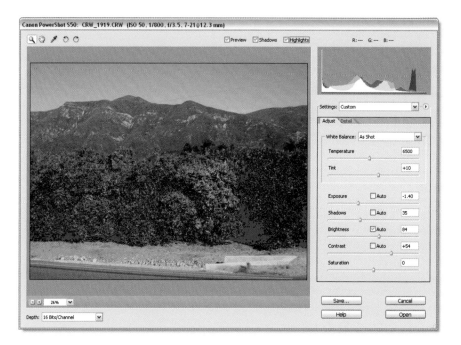

3. Again using the Organizer (Win) or Bridge (Mac), I double-clicked the image thumbnail to reopen it in the Camera RAW workspace. The plug-in automatically displays the last settings applied, so to return to the As Shot defaults, I chose Camera Raw Defaults from the Settings menu. Next I used the sliders to enhance the highlight information in the forefront bushes of the photo. I lowered the Shadows setting (moving the slider to the left), raised the Brightness setting (moving the slider to the right), and increased the Contrast (moving the slider right). The mountains are now even more overexposed—but again I can ignore that because I won't use them in the combined image. Now with the highlight information enhanced, I clicked Open to exit the plug-in dialog and open the image in the Elements workspace.

4. In order to combine these images in the Elements workspace, I first had to convert them from 16-bit to 8-bit, because Elements does not allow you to use layers with 16-bit images. With both images open, I converted each one by choosing Image > Mode > 8-Bits/Channel.

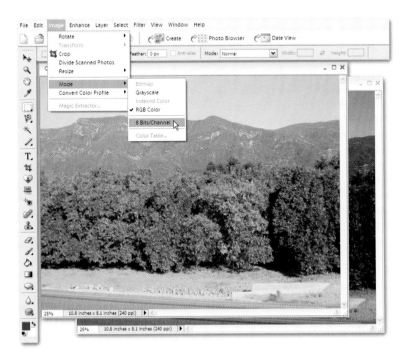

5. With the Move tool selected, I imported the highlight version of the photo into the shadow version using the drag-and-drop technique (see Chapter 4, "Mastering Layers"). Holding down Shift as I imported the image allowed me to place it in the exact center of the document. I renamed this layer "highlights."

6. To activate the Background (shadows) layer in the Layers palette, I pressed Alt/Option+[(left bracket). To gain access to a layer mask, I added a Levels adjustment layer by clicking the Adjustment layer icon and selecting Layers from the pop-up menu. As usual, I made no adjustments and simply closed the dialog by clicking OK. I then created a new group by Alt/Option-clicking between the highlight layer and the Levels adjustment layer in the Layers palette.

7. With the layer mask active, I pressed L to access the Lasso tool and made a loose selection around the bushes. I then added a feather to the selection by choosing Select > Feather, entering 100 pixels into the Feather Radius field, and clicking OK.

8. I then inverted the selection by choosing Select > Inverse. Pressing D to return to the application default colors of Black Foreground and White Background, I filled the selection with black by pressing Alt+Backspace (Win) or Option+ Delete (Mac). Since the filled selection was applied to the layer mask, it concealed all areas of the highlights layer except for the forefront bushes. I could now see through the masked areas to the enhanced shadow layer underneath. This resulted in a composite containing both enhanced shadow *and* highlight information.

9. Pressing B to access the Brush tool, I proceeded to choose a soft, large brush from the preset menu. Setting the brush to 30% Opacity in the options bar, I painted in the layer mask along the top edge of the bushes. Using a graphics pen and tablet with the Size and Opacity Brush Tablet Options enabled allowed me to blend the shadow and highlight layers together seamlessly.

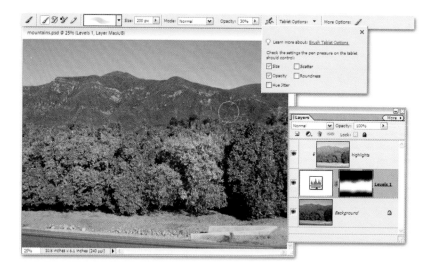

Combining Color Temperature

You can also use the Camera Raw plug-in to combine color temperature adjustments for different parts of an image and create a dramatic effect. As you did with the previous example, you must open a RAW file with the plug-in and then create two versions of the same image: one with accentuated warm colors, and one with accentuated cool colors. You can then convert both images to 8-bit mode and combine them using layers and layer masks.

The following example shows how I used the Camera Raw plug-in, along with layers and layer masks, to enhance the image shown in Figure 7.17 and combine color temperatures to create the version shown in Figure 7.18.

Figure 7.17
This skyline photo contains both cool and warm color temperatures.

Figure 7.18
Using Camera RAW, I enhanced the cool and warm color temperatures in separate versions of the image, which I then combined in Elements using layers and layer masks.

1. Using the Organizer (Win) or Bridge (Mac) file browser application, I located the RAW image, and opened it in the Camera RAW workspace by double-clicking its thumbnail. No previous adjustments were made, so I started out working with the As Shot camera default settings. I made sure to change the Depth setting in the lower-left corner of the dialog to 16 bits/channel in order to ensure that I was working with the widest possible color gamut.

2. Next I raised the Temperature setting (slider to the right) to enhance the warm colors in the sky portion of the photo. With the Highlight Clipping Option enabled, I kept my eye on the preview image as I adjusted the temperature, being careful not to fill the sky with any red dots, which indicate clipping. With the warm colors enhanced, I clicked Open to exit the plug-in dialog and open the image in the Elements workspace. I then chose File > Save As, renamed the image "sky," and saved it as a PSD file (Photoshop document).

3. Again using the Organizer (Win) or Bridge (Mac), I double-clicked the image thumbnail to reopen it in the Camera RAW workspace. The plug-in automatically displays the last settings applied, so to return to the As Shot defaults, I chose Camera Raw Defaults from the Settings menu. Next I lowered the Temperature setting (slider to the left) to enhance the cool colors in the cloud and water portions of the photo. Now with the cool colors enhanced, I clicked Open to exit the plug-in dialog and open the image in the Elements workspace.

4. In order to combine these images in the Elements workspace, I first had to convert them from 16-bit to 8-bit. With both images open, I converted each one by choosing Image > Mode > 8-Bits/Channel.

5. With the Move tool selected, I dragged and dropped the cool version of the photo into the warm version. Holding down Shift as I imported the image allowed me to place it in the exact center of the document. I renamed this layer "sky/water."

6. To activate the Background (shadows) layer in the Layers palette, I pressed Alt/Option+[(left bracket). To gain access to a layer mask, I added a Levels adjustment layer by clicking the Adjustment layer icon and selecting Layers from the pop-up menu. As usual, I made no adjustments and simply closed the dialog by clicking OK. I then created a new group by Alt/Option-clicking between the sky/water layer and the Levels adjustment layer in the Layers palette.

7. With the layer mask active, I pressed G to access the Gradient tool and proceeded to choose the Foreground to Transparent gradient from the default set in the Gradient Picker. Selecting the Reflected Gradient option in the options bar, I clicked and dragged in the center of the layer mask from the bottom of the clouds to just below the city shoreline. Since the gradient was applied to the layer mask, it revealed all areas of the cool image layer except for the sunset. I could now see through the masked area to the warm image layer underneath. This resulted in a composite containing both enhanced cool *and* warm colors.

Adding Filters, Styles, and Effects

Throughout the previous chapters, we've used many of the filters, styles, and preset effects that ship with Photoshop Elements 4, in the context of explaining how to use other tools when combining images. In this chapter, however, they will be our primary focus as we use them to add finishing touches to layered compositions. Just by including a simple drop shadow, border, outer glow, or all of the above, you can greatly add to your image's overall presentation. Elements offers a multitude of filters, styles, and effects to choose from, many of which can be applied with just one click of the mouse. With this chapter we'll take a look at creative ways to apply filters to your combined image projects.

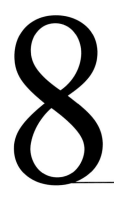

Chapter Contents

Filters and the Filter Gallery

In the days before digital image editors like Photoshop Elements, the only way to apply a filter to a photograph was to use special interchangeable camera lenses that allow you to tint or adjust a scene before capturing it to film. Nowadays in the digital age, you can use Photoshop Elements to apply filters to an image long after it is captured. And not only that, but the filters available in Elements allow you to do much more than just apply a tint or make a slight adjustment. In fact, you can change the focus, alter the color, distort the image, and even apply special effects (see Figure 8.1).

Original image

Filter > Blur > Radial Blur

Filter > Artistic > Poster Edges

Filter > Distort > Ocean Ripple

Figure 8.1 Some examples of applied filters

There are so many filter commands in Elements (over a hundred) that it would be impossible to describe each and every one in a single chapter. Figure 8.2 shows part of the Filter menu. The filter commands all produce different effects, and many of them contain different dialog options and controls. Some are easy to apply, while others are quite complicated. The best way to get familiar with them is through good old-fashioned experimentation. Apply a filter, play around with the settings in its dialog box, and use the preview to decide whether or not you like what you see.

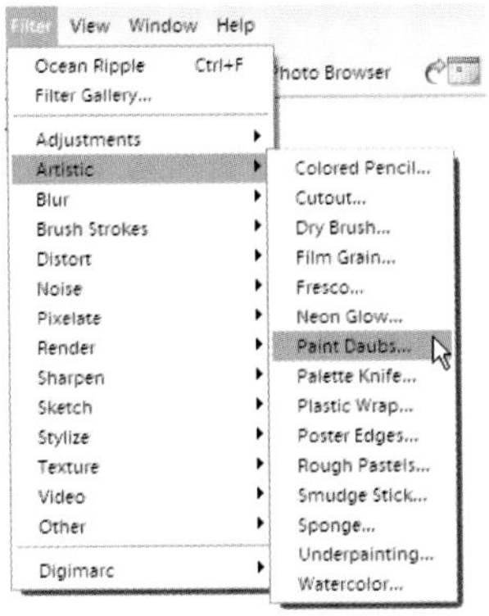

Figure 8.2

The Filter menu contains over 100 hundred commands organized by category into submenus. Shown here is the Artistic submenu.

As with most things in Elements, there's more than one way to incorporate filters into your work. These commands can be applied to individual image layers of your composition, or to the entire composition itself, once flattened. Here are just some of the ways you can use filters to enhance your combined image projects:

- Use the Texture commands to create textured layers and backgrounds (see the example "Image Effects" later in this chapter).

- Use the Blur commands to soften backgrounds and image layers, or to imply motion (see the "Creating Shadows and Softening Focus" example in Chapter 5, "The Power of Opacity and Blending").

- Use the Distort commands, such as Liquify, Spherize, or Wave, to distort image layers and type (see step 4 of the "Interactive Blend Modes" example in Chapter 5).

- Use the Artistic, Brush Strokes, and Sketch commands to give your composition a simulated natural media appearance (see the example "Filter Gallery Oil Paint Effect" later in this chapter).

- Sharpen your final composite (see the section "Applying Filters" later in this chapter).

Many of these filter effects are already set up for you in the Styles and Effects palette and can be applied with just one simple click of the mouse.

A Word of Warning

The biggest challenge when working with filters is maintaining the willpower not to overdo it. A lot of the filter effects can completely change the overall appearance of your image—*so use them with caution*. It's always best to use creative restraint and apply them tastefully.

Another caution is that filter effects, unlike the layer styles discussed later in the chapter, are not "live" or nondestructive, which means that once applied, they will permanently alter pixel information. The only way to reverse a filter effect is to apply the Edit > Undo command *before you close the file*.

To apply a filter to an entire composition, which usually contains multiple layers, the image must also be flattened. Therefore, to protect and preserve your pixels and layers, it's always a good idea to experiment with filters on a merged layer (see Figure 8.3) or on a duplicate, flattened version of your composition (see Chapter 4, "Mastering Layers") before saving your changes.

Figure 8.3 To preserve pixels and image layers for the sky/giraffe layered composition, I applied the Filter > Artistic > Watercolor effect to a merged layer at the top of the Layers palette.

Applying Filters

Filters can only be applied to a single selected layer in the Layers palette (not to multiple selected layers). Once the layer is targeted, filters can be applied to a selection made within the active layer, or if nothing is selected, to all of the pixels contained in that layer (see Figure 8.4).

You can apply a filter effect to the selected pixel area by choosing a command from the Filter menu. As we mentioned earlier, the menu contains over 100 hundred commands, all organized alphabetically by category and divided into submenus, as you saw in Figure 8.2. Each submenu is given a descriptive name, such as Artistic, Blur, or Distort. Elements displays any third-party filters (i.e., filters that you've purchased and installed separately) at the bottom of the menu.

Elements always displays the last used filter at the top of the Filter menu. To reapply the filter, press Ctrl+F (Windows) or ⌘+F (Mac).

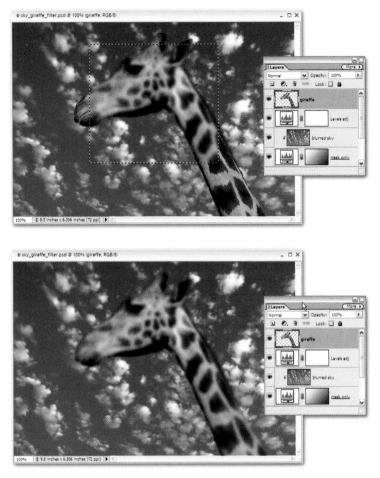

Figure 8.4

Top: With a selection made, applying Filter > Blur > Gaussian Blur affects only the pixels in the selected area of the giraffe layer. Bottom: With no selection made, the Blur filter is applied to every pixel on the giraffe layer.

You can also access the same categorized list of filter commands from the Filters section of the Styles and Effects palette. Double-click the filter thumbnail in the palette to display the options dialog for that filter.

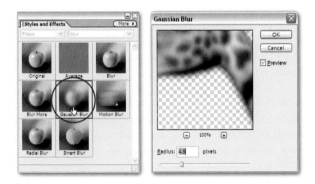

Note that some filters (e.g., Gaussian Blur) have their own options dialog, while others (such as all of the commands in the Artistic category) are controlled through the Filter Gallery dialog, like the Dry Brush filter shown here. Filter commands that are controlled via the Filter Gallery can also be accessed by choosing Filter > Filter Gallery, and selecting them from within the Gallery interface.

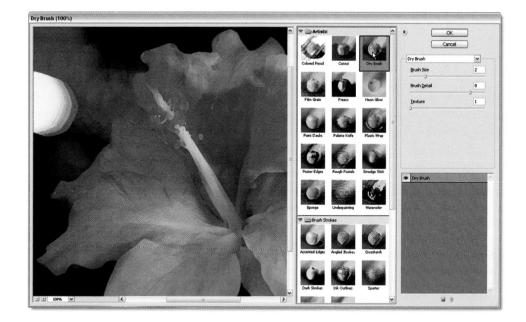

Example: Sharpening Your Final Composite

One of the most commonly applied focus effects is the Unsharp Mask filter, accessible under the Filter > Sharpen submenu. This filter, along with all of the other commands in the Sharpen set, allows you to enhance the focus of an image and make it appear sharper. It doesn't actually change the focus—only a camera lens can do that. But what it does do is detect the edges within an image and accentuate their contrast. The result is a trick of the eye that makes the image appear sharper. This is a great last step when preparing your composite image for final presentation, whether onscreen or in print.

Of all the Sharpen filter commands, the Unsharp Mask filter gives you the most control over the effect. Here's how the dialog works:

1. With a flattened version of your composition open (a merged layer or a flattened duplicate), access the Unsharp Mask dialog in one of two ways:

    • By choosing Filter > Sharpen > Unsharp Mask

    • By displaying the Styles and Effects palette (Window > Styles and Effects), selecting Filters from the Category menu, selecting Sharpen from the Library menu, and then double-clicking the Unsharp Mask thumbnail displayed in the palette, as shown here:

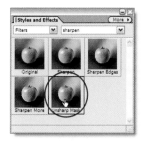

2. In the Unsharp Mask dialog, use the + and – zoom controls located below the image preview window to zoom in on a specific area of the image that needs sharpening. Note that with odd-numbered zoom percentages (33% and 67%), Elements does not interpolate the pixels, and as a result these views do not appear as smooth as they do at 50% and 100%. This can sometimes be misleading, and so it is best to view at either 50% or 100%. You can also hover over the preview area with the mouse to temporarily access the hand tool and reposition the image. Check the Preview option to see the effect applied to the entire image in the document window behind the dialog.

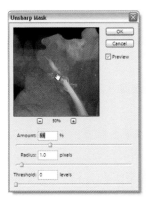

3. Drag the Amount slider to the right to raise the value to 200% or higher. This allows you to see the sharpening effect exaggerated in the preview. Click in the preview window and hold the mouse button down to see the image before sharpening; let up on the mouse button to see the effect after.

Before   After

4. Specify a radius amount using the slider. This value determines how much of the area surrounding the defined edges of the image will be affected. Lower values are more precise; higher values are more general.

1-pixel radius   10-pixel radius

What Radius Setting Should I Use?

The Radius setting for the Unsharp Mask filter should be determined by the final output destination of your image. As a general rule, lower values look best (the effect should be barely noticeable to the viewer), but this can vary depending on *how* the image will be viewed.

- For images intended for onscreen display (web pages, PDFs, PowerPoint presentations, etc.), enter the smallest value possible (e.g., 0.5 px).

- For medium-resolution printing, enter a radius of 1.0 to 2.0 pixels.

- For high-resolution printing, enter a radius amount of 2.0 or higher.

5. With the proper radius setting chosen for your image, lower the Amount value by dragging the slider to the left. Use the preview window to help determine the proper sharpening amount. Be careful not to *oversharpen* the image. Oversharpened images contain edges that are noticeably jagged, dark, and crisp.

Properly Sharpened Image   Oversharpened Image

6. In order to keep the image sharpened uniformly, it's best to leave the Threshold setting at 0. The Threshold setting is measured in luminosity levels and specifies the number of levels by which neighboring pixels must differ from each other in order to be recognized as an edge. A Threshold setting of 0 ensures uniformity when sharpening. Click OK to apply the sharpening effect.

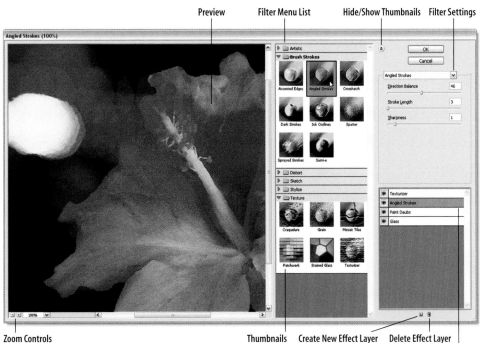

The Filter Gallery

The Filter Gallery allows you to choose from a select group of filter effects and apply several of them to an image at once. You can access the Filter Gallery by choosing it under the Filter menu or by choosing any filter that is handled by the gallery interface, such as the Artistic, Brush Strokes, or Sketch subsets.

As shown in Figure 8.5, the Filter Gallery dialog is made up of four sections: a preview area with zoom controls, a filter menu list (complete with descriptive thumbnails for every effect), a dynamic filter settings area, and a list of applied effect layers.

> **Note:** Don't confuse the effect layers in the Filter Gallery with the fill and adjustment layers you can create in the Layers palette, as described in Chapter 4. Read on for a complete description of the Filter Gallery's effect layers.

Preview   Filter Menu List   Hide/Show Thumbnails   Filter Settings

Zoom Controls   Thumbnails   Create New Effect Layer   Delete Effect Layer   Effect Layer Stack

Figure 8.5 The Filter Gallery dialog

Every time you open the Filter Gallery, a single effect layer is automatically created for you. Adding, deleting, and selecting effect layers in the Filter Gallery is similar to working with layers in the Layers palette (see Chapter 4). To add an effect you must first create an effect layer by clicking the Create New Effect Layer icon at the bottom of the dialog. Doing so duplicates the currently selected layer and positions it at the top of the effect layer stack. You can select an effect layer by clicking it, just as you would in the Layers palette; the only difference is that you can select only one effect layer at a time. The currently active effect layer is always highlighted gray (see Figure 8.6).

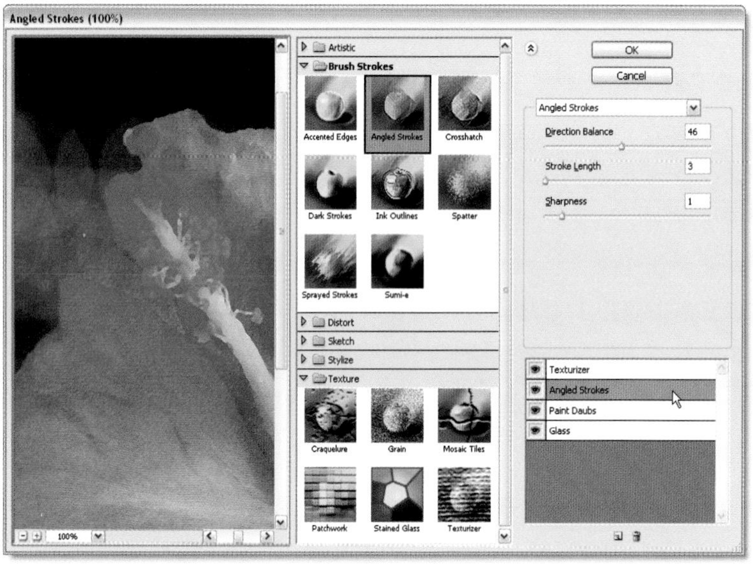

Figure 8.6
Selected effect layers are highlighted gray.

To delete an effect layer, select it from the stack and then click the trash icon at the bottom of the dialog. Note that you cannot drag an effect layer to the trash as you can when deleting layers in the Layers palette.

Note: To delete all of the effect layers at once, hold down Ctrl (Windows) or Command (Mac) to convert the Cancel button into a Default button. Then with Ctrl/Command held down, click Default to delete all of the layers. Click the Create a New Layer icon at the bottom of the dialog to try some different effects.

You can pick and choose which filter to apply to a selected effect layer by clicking on a thumbnail from the filter menu list. Click a folder (or the right-facing arrow to the left of it) to display all of the thumbnails in the filter set. Different filters contain different options. As you click thumbnails in the menu list, the settings to the right of the dialog change dynamically to display the available options for the chosen effect. For example, Figure 8.6 shows the settings available for the Angled Strokes filter. You can adjust the settings as needed to fine-tune the applied filter effect.

To add more effects, click the Create New Effect layer icon and click a different thumbnail from the menu. As you adjust the settings for added effect layers, notice how they interact with the settings applied to the effect layers positioned below. Repositioning the order of the layers can produce different results. Applying these filters using effect layers in the Filter Gallery is the only way to get them to interact in this way. Applying them separately without using effect layers does not produce the same effect.

You can adjust the settings for a selected effect layer at any time *before* clicking OK to close the dialog. Once you've closed the Filter Gallery, you cannot make further adjustments to the effect layers without first choosing Edit > Undo or clicking the Undo icon in the shortcuts bar.

Note: Elements always remembers the last applied settings every time the Filter Gallery is opened.

Example: Filter Gallery Oil Paint Effect

The following steps illustrate how you can use the Filter Gallery to convert your composite image into a digital oil painting. Except as specifically noted, the settings here should work with any image.

Note: The accompanying CD-ROM includes a video lesson on oil paint effects.

1. The first tweak this effect requires is to increase the saturation. Create a flat-tened version of your composition (either a merged layer or a flattened dupli-cate—see Chapter 4). Then, in the Layers palette, click the Adjustment layer icon and choose Hue/Saturation from the flyout menu. In the dialog, drag the Satura-tion slider to the right to increase the value and make the colors appear much more vivid. The amount of increased saturation you should apply depends on the image. If the image already contains bright colors, only increase the satura-tion level slightly (in the example shown here, the saturation level only needed to be raised to 15). If the image does not contain bright colors, increase the Satura-tion level to about 50 or higher. Remember, if you should accidentally over- or undersaturate the image, that's OK, because this is an adjustment layer, and you can always change the saturation setting *after* the Filter Gallery painting effect is applied. Click OK to close the dialog.

2. Now we can apply some filters, beginning with the image background. Press Alt+[(Windows) or Option+[(Mac) to select the Background layer. Under the Filter menu, choose Filter Gallery. In the Filter Gallery dialog, adjust the preview zoom amount and image positioning accordingly. Then click the Distort set, and click the Glass thumbnail. Set the Distortion amount to 3, set the Smoothness to 3, choose Canvas from the Texture pop-up menu, and set the scaling to 80% (as shown here). Don't click OK yet.

3. At the bottom of the Filter Gallery dialog, click the New Effect Layer icon (next to the trash can icon). Once you click the icon, a new effect layer containing the same filter effect as the initial layer is added to the top of the list. To change the filter effect that is applied to the new layer, click the Artistic set, and then click the Paint Daubs thumbnail. Set the Brush Size to 4, Sharpness to 1, and for Brush Type choose Simple (as shown here). We're still not done yet so don't click OK.

4. Click the New Effect Layer icon again to add another layer to the top of the list. This time click the Brush Strokes set, and then click the Angled Stroke thumbnail. Set the Direction Balance to 46, Stroke Length to 3, and Sharpness to 1. Nope. Still not done. Don't click OK yet.

5. Click the New Effect Layer icon one more time to add a fourth layer. To add a canvas-like texture to the combined filter effect, click the Texture set and click the Texturizer thumbnail. Choose Canvas from the Texture menu, set the Scaling to 65%, set Relief to 2, and for Light choose Top Left from the pop-up menu. Now click OK to apply all four filters to the image.

6. Duplicate this layer by pressing Ctrl+J (Windows) or ⌘+J (Mac). You should now have a duplicate layer positioned in between the Background Layer and the Hue and Saturation Adjustment layer in the Layers palette. Press Ctrl+Shift+U (Windows) or ⌘+Shift+U (Mac) to desaturate (remove all color from) the layer.

7. Rename the duplicate layer "Emboss," and change its blend mode to Overlay. The duplicate layer should now blend in and intensify the colors of the original layer positioned underneath it in the Layers palette, by darkening the darks and lightening the lights.

8. Choose Filter > Stylize > Emboss. In the dialog that appears, set the Angle amount to 135°, the Height to 1 pixel, and the Amount to 500% (as shown here), and click OK.

9. Finally, lower the opacity level of the Emboss layer so that the impasto effect does not appear too severe. In some instances you may want the effect to appear more noticeable, but if you're looking for a more natural appearance, try setting it to 50% or lower.

Layer Styles

Layer styles are similar to adjustment layers (and different from filters) in that they allow you to edit images dynamically. This means that you can apply editable effects to selected image, shape, or type layers without permanently altering any pixels. Because they work nondestructively, layer styles are referred to as "live effects." Some of these live effects include drop shadows, inner and outer glows, and bevels.

One thing that layer styles do have in common with filters is that they can be incorporated into your work in many different ways. You can apply styles to individual image layers of your composition, or to the entire composition itself once flattened.

Here are just some of the ways you can use styles to enhance your combined image projects:

- Apply the drop shadow or outer glow style to transparent image layers, to a selection, to type or shape layers, or to a flattened composite (see Figure 8.10 in the next section)

- Create colorful text/image composites by applying layer styles to shape and/or type layers (see step 6 in the section "Type Masks" in Chapter 6, "Compositing with Masks").

- Add a beveled border to a flattened version of a composite image (see "Framing Your Final Image" at the end of this chapter).

Applying Styles

To apply a style to a selected layer (or multiple selected layers), choose Window > Styles and Effects to display the Styles and Effects palette (see Figure 8.7).

At the top of the palette, choose Layer Styles from the menu on the left. Then, from the menu on the right, choose from a categorized list of available layer style sets. This menu is divided into two sections: the top half contains basic style sets that are entirely editable, such as Drop Shadows or Bevels; the bottom half contains more advanced style sets such as Glass Buttons or Patterns, where only certain options are editable (see Figure 8.8).

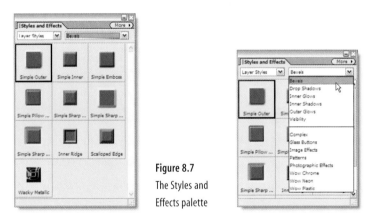

Figure 8.7
The Styles and Effects palette

Figure 8.8
The layer style category menu of the Styles and Effects palette

Note: In the Styles and Effects palette, the option that is chosen from the menu on the left (Layer Styles, Effects, or Filters) determines what options appear in the category menu on the right.

Once you choose a style category in the palette, a list of thumbnails appears, similar to what is seen in the Filter Gallery. Each thumbnail displays a visual example of what the style will look like once applied. Click a thumbnail to instantly apply the style to the selected layer(s) (see Figure 8.9).

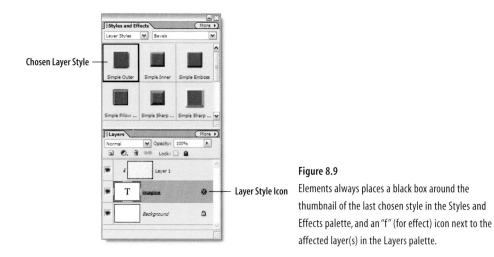

Chosen Layer Style

Layer Style Icon

Figure 8.9
Elements always places a black box around the thumbnail of the last chosen style in the Styles and Effects palette, and an "f" (for effect) icon next to the affected layer(s) in the Layers palette.

Keep in mind that multiple styles can be applied to a layer. For example, it's not unheard of to apply *both* a drop shadow *and* a bevel to a type or shape layer in a combined image project. Try experimenting with this by continuing to click thumbnails in the Styles and Effects palette (see Figure 8.10).

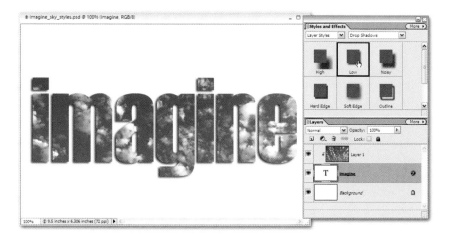

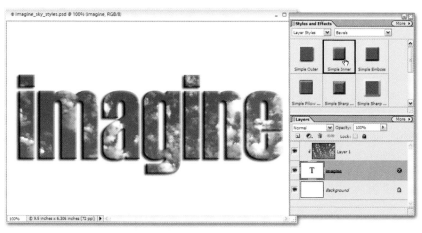

Figure 8.10 Top: A type layer clipping mask with a Low drop shadow applied; Bottom: The same type layer with the Low drop shadow *and* a Simple Inner bevel applied

Editing Styles

Basic style attributes can be edited *after* they are applied. You can do so using the Style Settings dialog. To access the dialog, select the layer containing the applied style and choose Layer > Layer Style > Style Settings, or just double-click the layer style "f" icon in the Layers palette (see Figure 8.11).

Figure 8.11

Double-click the layer style "f" icon in the Layers palette to access the Style Settings dialog.

Style Limitations

Unlike Photoshop CS2, Elements does not allow you to save and load custom style settings. This means that you cannot permanently change and save the default settings for a style, as you can with brushes or gradients. Also, not all style attributes in Elements can be edited once they've been applied to a layer, as they can in Photoshop CS2. Only the attributes available in the Style Settings dialog can be edited.

In the Style Settings dialog you can adjust the settings for effect lighting, shadow distance, inner and outer glow size, bevel size, and bevel direction. As you adjust the settings in the dialog, check the Preview box to see your edits in the document window. Click OK to apply.

Copying Styles

Since you can't save your own custom style settings in Elements, the best way to apply edited styles is to copy them. There are two ways you can do this:

*   In the Layers palette, select the layer that contains the style you'd like to copy. Then choose Copy Layer Style from the Layer > Layer Style submenu or from the contextual menu (Windows: right-click the layer; Mac: Control-click the layer). Select the layer you'd like to apply the style to and choose Paste Layer Style from the Layer > Layer Style submenu or from the contextual menu.

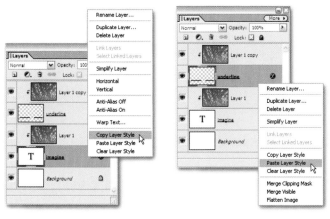

Copy Layer Style   **Paste Layer Style**

- Alt-drag (Windows) or Option-drag (Mac) the layer style "f" icon from the styled layer to another layer in Layers palette.

Clearing Styles

I encourage you to experiment with layer styles. Add several of them to a layer, try tweaking their settings, and see what happens. After a short while, you'll soon find that manipulating live effects can become addicting. It's very easy to overdo it. Eventually you'll reach a point where you just want to start over. Thankfully, the Clear Styles command allows you to delete any applied styles and start fresh.

There are two ways to apply the command:

- In the Layers palette, select the layer containing the styles you'd like to delete. Then choose Clear Layer Style from the Layer > Layer Style submenu or the contextual menu (Windows: right-click the layer; Mac: Control-click the layer). As soon as you apply the command, the effects disappear immediately from the document window, as does the Layer Style icon in the Layers palette.

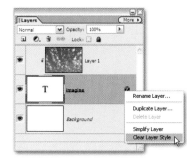

Note: Right-click (Windows) or Control-click (Mac) the Layer Style icon to access the Clear Layer Style command from a much shorter contextual menu.

- Click and drag the layer style "f" icon from the layer to the trash icon at the top of the Layers palette. As soon as you let up on the mouse button, the layer style effects disappear immediately from the document window.

Simplifying Layers

Elements also allows you to convert "live" layer style effects into pixels, thereby rendering them uneditable. In most cases, it's best to leave your effects editable and not convert them. However, to prevent another artist from changing your effects—let's say for an advertising piece that you're sending to another publication—you can always apply the Simplify Layer command.

The Simplify Layer command is only accessible through the Layers palette. Select the layer you'd like to convert, and then choose Simplify Layer from the Layers palette menu or the contextual menu (Right-click the layer (Windows) or Control-click the layer (Mac).) As soon as you apply the command, the Layer Style icon disappears from the layer in the Layers palette and the effect is no longer editable.

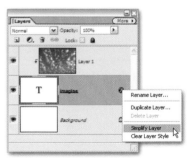

Note: You can also apply the Simplify Layer command to type and shape layers. Doing so converts them into pixels, thereby rendering them uneditable.

Effects

Effects in Elements are made up of filters and layer styles. The good thing about effects is that they can be applied quickly and easily. The bad thing is that they are not all editable (only applied attributes in the Style Settings dialog can be adjusted), and most of them are not very impressive. What's even more frustrating is that you can't create and save your own custom effects.

However, you can still use effects to your advantage. I like to use them to create custom frames quickly and easily. They can also come in handy when working with text/image composites. In this last section, we'll take a look at how you can use effects to add a finishing touch to your combined image projects.

Applying Effects

To apply an effect to a selected layer (you *cannot* apply effects to multiple selected layers), choose Window > Styles and Effects to display the Styles and Effects palette. At the top of the palette, choose Effects from the menu on the left. Then from the menu on the right, choose from a categorized list of available effect sets. Options include frames, image effects, text effects, and textures. There is also an option to view all of the effects at once in the palette.

Once you choose an effect category in the palette, a list of thumbnails appears, similar to the one in the Filter Gallery. Each thumbnail displays a visual example of what the effect will look like once applied (see Figure 8.12).

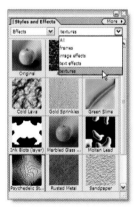

Figure 8.12
Choose an effect category to view its thumbnails in the Styles and Effects palette.

To apply an effect, click and drag a thumbnail from the palette directly onto the layer in the Layers palette, or double-click a thumbnail. Either method instantly applies the effect to the selected layer. You can apply effects to a portion of a layer by making a selection first, and then double-clicking or dragging the thumbnail.

Note: Many of these effects require that the image be flattened before they can be applied. To preserve your layered composition, be sure to apply these effects to a duplicate, flattened version of the document.

Example: Altering Image Effects

The image effects category offers a wide variety of visual interpretations that you can apply to your compositions, from the more practical and attractive (soft focus) to the outright bizarre (fluorescent chalk). In most cases you won't be satisfied with the built-in effect; you'll want to tweak it. But because these effects are not "live," they cannot be edited on the fly. This exercise shows how to get around this limitation by using a layer mask and some brushwork to manipulate an image effect after applying it.

1. Create a duplicate, flattened version of your composition (if you're not sure how to do this, see Chapter 4). Choose Window > Styles and Effects to display the Styles and Effects palette. At the top of the dialog, choose Effects from the menu on the left. Then from the menu on the right, choose Image Effects. Double-click the Colorful Center thumbnail to apply that effect. In the document window, your image should gradate from color to black and white from the center outward.

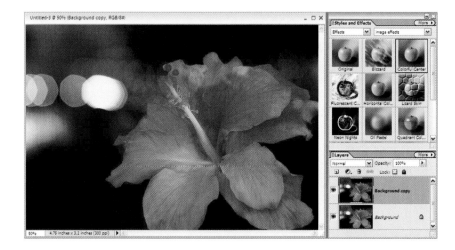

2. The effect is interesting, but only as a starting point. In this example, I like the idea of keeping the flower in color, but stripping all the color out of the background. To make this happen, you first need to select the Background layer by pressing Alt+[(Windows) or Option+[(Mac). Then click the adjustment layer icon at the top of the Layer palette and choose Levels from the pop-up menu. When the Levels dialog appears, click OK to close it. The purpose of adding the Levels adjustment layer is to gain access to its companion layer mask, not to make an actual adjustment.

3. Alt-click (Windows) or Option-click (Mac) between the new Levels adjustment layer and the top layer in the Layers palette to create a clipping mask.

4. Press B to access the Brush tool, and select a soft brush from the options bar. Set the brush opacity pretty low to start out with—say about 30%. Press D to reset the default colors to black foreground and white background, and then click the layer mask thumbnail in the Layers palette. Paint around the object that you would like to remain in color (the flower in this example). If you're using a graphics pen and tablet, try enabling the Shape and Opacity Tablet Options in the options bar to help you paint with a more natural feel.

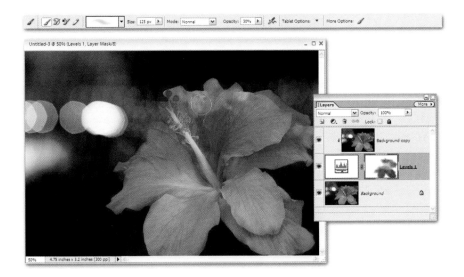

5. When you've finished bringing the color back into your image, click the top layer in the Layers palette and then press O to access the Sponge tool. In the options bar, make sure that Mode is set to Desaturate. Choose a soft brush, size it appropriately, and then paint away the color areas of the background. When you're done, you should have an image that looks something like the example shown here.

Some of you may be wondering why we used the Colorful Center effect at all, if we were going to modify it as much as we did. Wouldn't it be more straightforward to start by dcsaturating the top layer? The answer is that by applying the initial effect in step 1 you are saving yourself some brushwork in achieving the final result in step 5. Using the effect as a starting point is faster and easier than starting from scratch.

Example: Textures and Type Masks

Textures are some of the better effects available in Elements. By double-clicking a texture thumbnail in the Styles and Effects palette, you can generate a custom texture in seconds. With this exercise, we'll take a look at how to incorporate texture effects into a type mask. For our project example, we'll revisit the "imagine" project first seen in Chapter 6.

1. Press Ctrl+N (Windows) or Cmd+N (Mac) to access the New document dialog. Create a new RGB document that is 9.5 × 6.3 inches at 220 ppi. Be sure to choose the default white background color for the background contents. Click OK to close the dialog and create the document.

2. Press T to access the Horizontal Type tool. In the tool's options bar, select a bold face font with characters that are thick enough for a texture placed within them to be recognizable, as well as a large point size and an alignment option. In the example, I've chosen Haettenschweiler on the Windows platform, 282 pt, centered. Click in the center of the document window and type your text ("imagine" in the example). As soon as you begin typing, a new text layer is added to the document above the Background layer. Click the Move tool icon in the Tools palette and center the text in the document window. Notice that the name of the type layer in the Layers palette automatically displays what was typed.

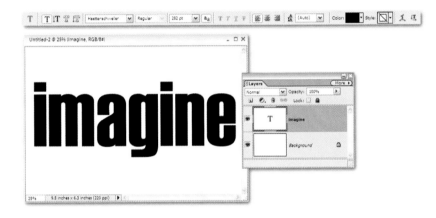

3. Choose Window > Styles and Effects to display the Styles and Effects palette. At the top of the dialog, choose Effects from the menu on the left. Then from the menu on the right, choose textures. Double-click the Psychedelic Strings thumbnail to apply that effect. The texture should generate itself on a new layer above the type.

4. Alt-click (Windows) or Option-click (Mac) between the new texture layer and the type layer in the layers palette to create a clipping mask. The texture will be automatically cropped inside the text characters. If you'd like, you can select the texture layer and reposition it inside the letters with the Move tool. Rename the layer "texture."

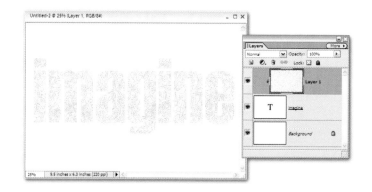

5. Press Alt+[(Windows) or Option+[(Mac) to select the type layer underneath in the Layers palette. Then at the top of the Styles and Effects palette, choose Layer Styles from the menu on the left and Wow Plastic from the menu on the right. Click the Wow Plastic Aqua Blue thumbnail to apply the layer style to the type.

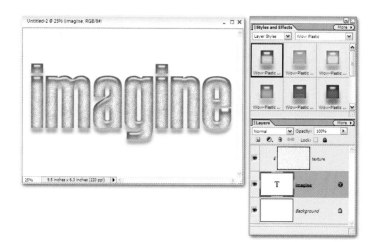

6. The finished result should look something like this. Because the Wow Plastic Aqua Blue style contains transparency, you can see the masked texture through the rounded letters. Pretty cool, don't you think?

> **Note:** To view a layer without all of its applied layer style effects, choose Layer > Layer Style > Hide All Effects. To make the styles visible again, choose Show All Effects under the same menu.

Framing Your Final Image

Elements also offers frame effects that allow you to generate a frame and apply it to a flattened version of your composite image. To find them, choose Frames from the drop-down list in the Styles and Effects palette. Most of the frames can be applied by simply double-clicking or dragging the thumbnail over the Background layer (Figure 8.13), while others require that a selection be made first (Figure 8.14).

Figure 8.13 The Photo Corners frame can be applied to a flattened version of your image by double-clicking the thumbnail in the Styles and Effects palette.

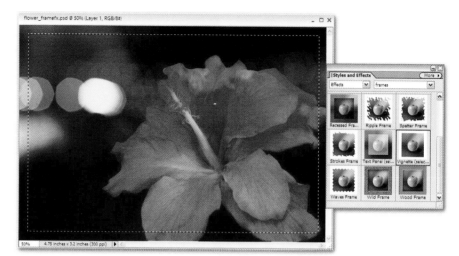

Selection Made Before Applying the Vignette Frame Effect

After Applying the Vignette Frame Effect

Figure 8.14 The Vignette frame requires that you make a selection to indicate the crop area before applying the effect: (top) a selection made before applying the Vignette frame effect; (bottom) the result of applying the Vignette frame effect.

Exercise: Creating a Custom Frame

While frame effects are easily applied, they don't always generate spectacular results. If you like the idea of framing your final composite image—possibly for use on a website gallery or an onscreen presentation—you may want to consider creating your own frame using texture effects and layer styles. The following exercise shows how you can create a custom wood frame effect.

1. Create a duplicate, flattened version of your composition (if you're not sure how to do this, see Chapter 4). Choose Window > Styles and Effects to display the Styles and Effects palette. At the top of the dialog, choose Effects from the menu on the left.

2. At the top of the Styles and Effects palette, choose image textures from the menu on the right. Double-click the Wood - Rosewood thumbnail to apply the effect. The texture should generate itself on a new layer above the Background layer. Rename this layer "wood frame."

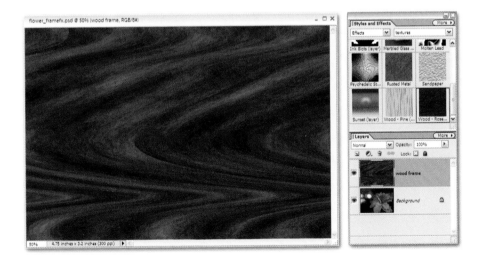

3. Press D to ensure that the application default colors are set to black foreground and white background, then choose Image > Resize > Canvas Size. In the Canvas Size dialog, check the Relative option and enter .25 inches in both the Width and Height fields. Make sure the Canvas Extension Color option is set to Background Color.

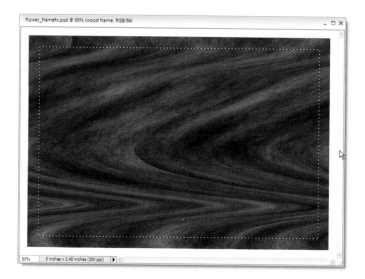

4. Ctrl-click (Windows) or ⌘-click (Mac) the wood frame layer to make a selection of it. Choose Select > Modify > Contract and enter 50 pixels in the dialog that appears. Click OK to close the dialog and contract the selection.

5. Press the Backspace (Windows) or Delete (Mac) key to remove the selected portion of the wood frame layer. Press Ctrl+D (Windows) or ⌘+D (Mac) to deselect. Then, at the top of the Styles and Effects palette, choose Layer Styles from the menu on the left and Bevels from the menu on the right. Click the Simple Inner thumbnail to apply the layer style to the wood frame.

6. Back in the Styles and Effects palette, choose Drop Shadows from the category menu on the right. Click the Low thumbnail to apply the layer style. Doing so adds some more depth and realism to the overall effect.

7. Double-click the layer style "f" icon in the Layers palette to access the Style Settings dialog. For this image, changing the Shadow Distance setting to 16px and the Bevel size to 10px gives it a more realistic appearance. Feel free to use your own discretion with an image of your own. Click OK to close the dialog and apply the change.

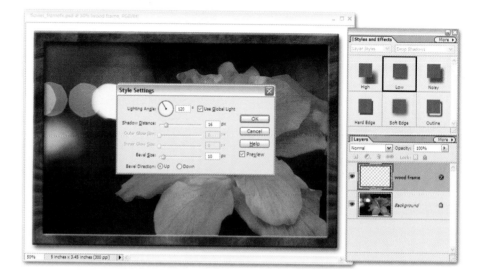

8. Ctrl-click (Windows) or ⌘-click (Mac) the wood frame layer to make a selection of it. To change the color of the frame, click the adjustment layer icon at the top of the Layers palette and choose Hue and Saturation from the pop-up menu. When the dialog appears, increase the Hue setting to +4, decrease the Saturation setting to -40, and decrease the Lightness setting to -33. These settings give the wood frame a much darker appearance. Check the Preview option to see the change in the document as you make your adjustment. Click OK to apply.

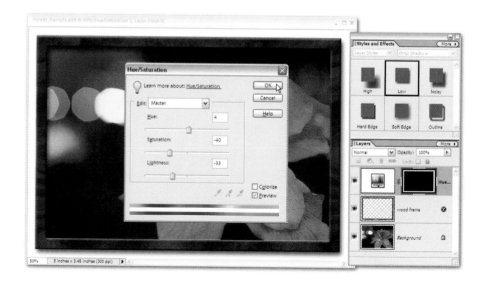

9. The finished result should look similar to the example shown here. You can change the color of the custom frame at any time by adjusting the settings in the Hue and Saturation adjustment layer dialog.

Index

Note to the Reader: Throughout this index **boldfaced** page numbers indicate primary discussions of a topic. *Italicized* page numbers indicate illustrations.